Postmodern Youth Ministry

Exploring Cultural Shift

Creating Holistic Connections

Cultivating Authentic Community

Tony Jones

Youth Specialties

ZondervanPublishingHouse
Grand Rapids, Michigan

A Division of HarperCollinsPublishers

Postmodern Youth Ministry: Exploring cultural shift, creating holistic connections, cultivating authentic community

Copyright © 2001 by Youth Specialties

Youth Specialties Books, 300 S. Pierce St., El Cajon, CA 92020,
are published by Zondervan Publishing House,
5300 Patterson Ave. S.E., Grand Rapids, MI 49530.

Library of Congress Cataloging-In-Publication Data

Jones, Tony, 1968-
    Postmodern youth ministry : exploring cultural shift, creating holistic
connections, cultivating authentic community / Tony Jones.
        p. cm.
    Includes bibliographical references and index.
    ISBN 0-310-23817-X
    1. Church work with youth. 2. Postmodernism – Religious
aspects – Christianity. I. Title.

    BV4447 .J664 2001
    259'.23–dc21

                                                        00-043935

Edited by Linnea Lagerquist and Dave Urbanski
Cover and interior design by Proxy in conjunction with M Studios

Printed in the United States of America

01 02 03 04 05 06 07 / CH / 10 9 8 7 6 5 4 3 2 1

Dedicated to Tanner Hawthorne Jones

the beginning of whose life will forever be tied to this book

and to his mother and my best friend, Julie

About the Contributors

Rudy Carrasco pastors Latino and African American young people at the Harambee Christian Family Center in Pasadena, California, where he is associate director. Rudy and Harambee's executive director, Derek Perkins, frequently consult on racial reconciliation, social issues, and urban community development for both Christian and secular groups and publications.

Brad Cecil pastors the Axxess church-within-a-church at Pantego Bible Church in Arlington, Texas. He's founder and president of Brad Cecil and Associates (marketing and development consultants specializing in nonprofits) and is a frequent conference speaker and consultant. Brad is a former youth speaker and evangelist for Word of Life Fellowship and former director of YMCA Casa Shelter for homeless and runaway youth.

Mark Driscoll pastors Seattle's Mars Hill Fellowship, a church he planted in 1996. He also cohosts *Sweet Talk*, a national radio show, as well as consults and lectures around the United States on postmodernity, the arts, generations, and cultural shifts.

Dan Kimball is the pastor of the Graceland church-within-a-church at Santa Cruz (California) Bible Church, which is designed for postmodern generations. He served as youth pastor at Santa Cruz Bible Church for seven years before starting Graceland in 1997.

Brian McLaren is author of *The Church on the Other Side, Finding Faith,* and *A New Kind of Christian*. He's also senior pastor of Cedar Ridge Community Church in the Baltimore-Washington area, serves on several boards, and is active in the Terra Nova Project through Youngleader Networks (youngleader.net/terranova.html).

Sally Morgenthaler is author of *Worship Evangelism: Inviting Unbelievers into the Presence of God*, on-site worship consultant for Denver Seminary, and creative design director for Pathways Church in Denver, Colorado. She's founder and president of SJM Management Co. and speaks and consults on issues of worship and postmodern culture.

Doug Pagitt is a graduate of Bethel Seminary and is pastor of Solomon's Porch – a holistic, missional Christian community in Minneapolis. Doug hosts a Web site called wonderings.com, where innovative ideas are born and shared exclusive of the publishing industry.

Kara Powell is assistant professor at Azusa (California) Pacific University and assistant junior high pastor at Lake Avenue Church in Pasadena, California. She has written many articles and books, including *Good Sex: A Whole-Person Approach to Teenage Sexuality and God* (Youth Specialties).

Leonard Sweet is a postmodern expert who knows and understands the distinctives of this cultural shift and how the church should respond. He's author of *SoulTsunami* and *AquaChurch: Essential Leadership Arts for Piloting Your Church in Today's Fluid Culture*.

Pete Ward teaches in the masters degree program in youth ministry at Kings College in London, England. He's written several books, most recently *God at the Mall*, among other articles for youth workers in the U.K. He resides in Cold Ash, Berkshire.

Mike Yaconelli is owner of Youth Specialties and a passionate, provocative speaker whose messages are marked by his infectious love for Jesus. He speaks around the world and pastors a small church in northern California. His latest book among many is *Dangerous Wonder: The Adventure of Childlike Faith*.

Contents

Preface

This work is the ink-on-paper version of thoughts I've been wrestling with for a dozen years. As I journeyed through college and seminary, my desire to be a youth pastor seemed to wane – I didn't know what I had to give to students. And whatever I had to give, it sure wasn't anything new. Well, I found out that God doesn't really need me to reinvent the gospel, he just wants me to share it with students.

In the same way, nothing here is particularly new. Instead, this is an attempt to take some of the most innovative thoughts of the postmodern movement and apply them to the practice of youth ministry. Of the extent to which this is a success, you, the reader, are the judge. In some ways, I'm sure I have betrayed the tenets of postmodernism, and in others the principles of youth ministry. In either case, it's only my inability to grasp the concepts involved that's to blame, not the fault of anyone mentioned below.

My thanks go to Professor Edward Bradley of Dartmouth College whom God used to foster my intellectual life and who was a faithful reader of this manuscript. While at Fuller Seminary, I was mentored and shaped by the late Bob Guelich, the late Jim McLendon, Miroslav Volf, and Nancey Murphy. Professor Murphy is, more than anyone, responsible for my understanding of postmodernism.

More recently my thoughts have been shaped by the men and women of the Terra Nova Project of Leadership Network, a group committed to engaging the emerging postmodern revolution in thought and culture. Mark Oestreicher, Tic Long, Mike Yaconelli, and Dave Urbanski at Youth Specialties have been encouraging and resourceful during this project.

I also must thank the staff, congregation, and especially the youth of the Colonial Church of Edina who have allowed me the space to work out many of these ideas and who have given me the time to write a book. Special thanks go to my co-youth workers Danielle Hample, Megan Hughes, and Tim Inman, and to our senior pastor David Fisher. My parents, also members of Colonial, have been a constant source of encouragement. Shane Hipps, a most loyal friend, has been the most faithful reader of this manuscript, and his thoughts have shaped what you hold in your hands.

Above all, my wife Julie gets the credit for making me into a better person than I am. Many nights she told me that I could indeed write a book, and many mornings she kicked me out of bed and told me to go do it! Not only that, she gave birth and began to raise a son without enough help from me. Bless you, Julie.

Soli Deo Gloria!

Tony Jones

Advent, 2000

The Day My World Changed

It was the summer between college and seminary. I was at the family lake cabin, and the dinner-table conversation turned to topics theological. Seated there was a fairly new family friend who was between her junior and senior years at college. She took umbrage at my confidence in the Christian faith, so she and I continued to talk even as the others did dishes.

I really thought I had it all lined up: I had been trained by the best Christian apologists at my secular university campus. I knew the Four Laws. But I knew this was going to be tough, so I brought out the young evangelist's trump card: C. S. Lewis.

There is a tri-lemma, I told my new friend. "Upon examining the claims of Christ," I boldly said, "we must declare him either the Lord, a liar, or a lunatic."

"Well, I believe he is Lord *for you*," came the response.

"I must not have explained myself," I said. "He claimed not just to be Lord for Tony but for all humanity — in fact, for all creation."

"That's fine. I believe that *for you*, he is Lord of all creation."

"But he claims to be Lord of all creation *for everyone*."

"Okay, *for you* he's Lord of all creation for everyone."

I chuckled sympathetically when I read Tony's story about C. S. Lewis' famous trilemma (Lord, Liar, or Lunatic) not working during the dinnertime conversation. If Lewis were writing today, he'd have to mention a fourth alliterated alternative: Legend. For postmoderns who've watched their share of History Channel documentaries on "the historical Jesus" and read the findings of the Jesus Seminar, the most obvious answer to the question, "Who is Jesus?" is "Who knows?" They see Christian accounts of Jesus' life as hopelessly distorted by the legends that seem to grow up around all extraordinary historical figures. So logically cornering folks into confessing Christ as Lord isn't such a great strategy anymore.

Brian McLaren

I wish I could say I had a great comeback or I gracefully bowed out of the conversation at that point. But unfortunately, I did not. Instead I groped for answers and counterpoints. I argued that much of Western philosophy is based on the syllogism, and that when something is proven, it demands universal consent. In the end, I did far more harm to that friend's soul than I should have – and I looked like a buffoon doing it.

But no one had told me that the rules had changed. It was as if she had been playing golf and I had been playing football. What happened in a little cabin in the north woods of Minnesota was an aftershock of an earthquake that has changed the landscape of academia and is currently rocking Western culture. Many call it the most important cultural shift in 500 years; some call it the Second Reformation.

Most commonly it's called postmodernism.

POSTMODERNISM:
Of or relating to art, architecture, or literature that reacts against earlier modernist principles, as by reintroducing traditional or classical elements of style or by carrying modernist styles or practices to extremes: "the postmodern mode of tapering the tops of buildings" (Jane Holtz Kay).

I strongly believe that the postmodern shift we are currently experiencing will be with us for a long time and that the world will never be the same. And I believe that we, the youth workers of the church, have an incredible opportunity to lead the church into the future. While most of our bosses are beholden to the methods of the past, we are immersed in the postmodern world.

I've heard recently that postmodernity is just another fad consuming the conference circuit that will soon pass. I totally disagree. Tony is right that postmodernity is the most significant cultural shift we've seen in the last 500 years. It's not a generational issue exclusive to Gen-X or Millennials. In fact, it's fast becoming the adopted epistemology of all adults. Everyone in ministry — not just youth and young adult pastors — will have to wrestle with this phenomenon.

Brad Cecil

And God may call upon us, the youth workers, to be the prophets within his church, to wake it from its modernistic slumber.

Are You Ready?

Recently, the giant computer networking device firm Cisco Systems launched a series of television ads. The venues quickly move to different places on the globe, with individuals of different ages and ethnicities all stating phrases that are seamlessly edited to form a unified statement. These are the texts of two of the ads:

There are seven new people on the Internet every second. Every fourth person on the Web is buying something right now. This month around one billion dollars will be spent. One day, there won't be any paper money. Are you ready? Are you ready? Are you ready? Are you ready? [1]

The Web had more users in its first five years than the telephone did in the first thirty. A population the size of the United Kingdom joins the Internet every six months. One day the Internet will make long distance calls a thing of the past. Are you ready? Are you ready? Are you ready? Are you ready? [2]

Yes, the world is changing at a dramatic pace. Within the cultural changes we see every day in ads like these is a change in the very heart of philosophy, language theory, and epistemology. While youth pastors may be tempted to focus more on superficial cultural changes, it is imperative that we peel back the cultural layers and examine the academic heart of this postmodern shift.

Sorry. No Models Inside...

This book will *not* give you a model for your youth ministry. That is not my purpose. I do not have the largest youth group in my area, and I'm not trying to sell you a system or a paradigm. There are no follow-up workbooks. (There is, however, a supplemental Web site with spiritual exercises and activities. Visit www.YouthSpecialties.com/free/pmym.)

Instead of promoting a new paradigm, we must deconstruct the old paradigms and then propose a series of reflections on culture, the church, and the state of youth ministry as we begin the third millennium. The anecdotes I use from my own ministry or someone else's are *not models* but stories that attempt to put flesh on a concept.

The new paradigm will be up to you. That's because what works in my town probably won't work in yours. Do not be disheartened by that; instead you might sense real freedom. Your denomination doesn't know what will work best in your context, and neither does a megachurch three states away. Only by discerning prayer and God-given wisdom and humility will we be able to enter the culture our students live in as *missionaries.* And then *you and I*, in different ways in different contexts, will be able to devise programs, events, and ministry plans that will best minister to those students.

Why take this postmodern shift seriously? Because more and more of our students are seeing the world with postmodern eyes. And because when they head off to college and into adult life, they're entering a postmodern world. Professors and MTV may deconstruct their modern thinking, but they dare not deconstruct our students' faith. We can help students to see how faith can survive — even thrive — in a postmodern world.

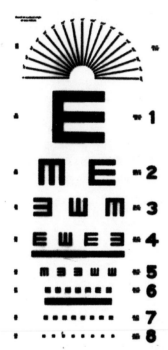

Postmodernism is a big word and a big concept. Many believe it's the most profound societal change since the Enlightenment. In this chapter, we will explore the dénouement of modernism and the birth of postmodernism, the differences between the two, and some of the cultural implications — and implications for youth ministry — this movement is creating.

postmodernism

1

What is real?

This is not a new query. Philosophers, theologians, and all of humanity have been asking this question as long as we have been able to formulate questions.

Plato, a philosopher who lived in the fifth and fourth centuries B.C., taught about a group of people sitting in a cave believing that the flickering shadows on the walls were the deepest reality. One of their number left the cave and saw the sunlight and other people who were the cause of the shadows, and he returned to the cave to tell his friends. Not convinced, they killed him — they could not comprehend nor convey that someone (namely, a philosopher) could discover a "more real" reality than they could see.

Do you remember when you first wrapped your mind around this question? I was in grade school and someone suggested to me that maybe our entire lives were merely another being's dream. That blew my second-grade mind!

16

This analogy is perfect. For the last few years I've had a cartoon depicting the Plato's cave analogy hanging next to my desk. It's a constant reminder that I may not be totally crazy when I find myself mumbling and stumbling for words when asked why we do certain things differently at Graceland — or responding to questions with precise words about what postmodernism is and explaining that change truly is happening and a new culture is emerging.

Dan Kimball

The Enlightenment and Modernism

Many centuries after Plato, René Descartes (1596-1650) fired another major salvo in this battle over reality. The Enlightenment was a time of great intellectual growth following the rediscovery of classical thought and art in the Renaissance. The Enlightenment project was meant to show that human beings were kings of the universe, and, although God was still a major player, many thinkers were out to show that human beings are not dependent upon him.[3]

17

In its broadest sense, foundationalism is merely the acknowledgment of the seemingly obvious observation that not all beliefs we hold (or assertions we formulate) are on the same level, but that some beliefs (or assertions) receive their support from other beliefs (or assertions) that are more "basic" or "fundamental."

Stanley Grenz and John Franke, *Beyond Foundationalism: Shaping Theology in a Postmodern* Context, 29

18

Descartes is most famous for his formula *cogito ergo sum*: "I think, therefore I am." By this he meant that our existence, yours and mine, is provable by and dependent upon our ability to doubt and reason. That is, we are not dependent on anything we cannot prove — a divine being, for instance. This is the genesis of foundationalism: the methodology by which one breaks everything down to its most fundamental components and builds up from there. (And yes, that is where fundamentalism comes from.)

Following Descartes, a group of British philosophers called the empiricists moved away from deductive reasoning as the foundation of knowledge and instead based their system on sensory impressions. And subsequently the "logical positivists" made sensory experience the indubitable foundation. [4]

Whether the foundation is an absolute belief that cannot be questioned or simply the sensory experience of an individual human being, the foundation is one of fact. Something absolute — experience or knowledge — is considered the "truth" and the basis of all thought.

Descartes also changed the starting point for people. Instead of starting in belief, Descartes suggests that we must start in doubt, then the only things to be believed are the things proven to be absolutely certain. In modernity everyone becomes a skeptic because that's the "higher ground." It has been intriguing to see children — who naturally adopt belief as their starting point — grow up and be trained to adopt doubt as the higher ground. It reminds me of the words of Christ — "except you become as little children."

Brad Cecil

For example, a Christian foundation might be Scripture – most of the framework of Christianity is built on the Bible. A foundationalist Christian might even say that *everything* – all Christian belief and practice – is based on the Bible.

Structurally, such a system might look like this:[5]

PRACTICE
THEOLOGY
SCRIPTURE

19

The Enlightenment scientists who came after Descartes built upon his foundation with the newfound belief that everything is ultimately knowable by the all-powerful human mind. The universe was quantified into laws of physics (*laws*, not theories), the celestial realm was figured out, and it no longer needed a God turning a crank to keep it moving.

Thus the Modern Era was born.

If there was an underlying credo of modernity, it might have been, "It's good to be king!" Human beings finally stood as the crown of God's creation – even at the cost of discarding God himself. The birth of modern machines and technology gave rise to the Industrial Revolution. Protestantism, a branch of Christianity predicated on every believer's ability to work out an individual relationship with God, flourished. And humankind seemed to be on the brink of making God an irrelevant concept.

The Birth of Postmodernism

Frederick Nietzche (1844-1900) understood this trend. His famous declaration, "God is dead," began a movement that's at the heart of postmodernism: *deconstruction.*

DECONSTRUCTION:
A philosophical movement and theory of literary criticism that questions traditional assumptions about certainty, identity, and truth, asserts that words can only refer to other words, and attempts to demonstrate how statements about any text subvert their own meanings.

20

There are three umpires hanging out after a baseball game. The premodern umpire says, "There are balls, and there are strikes, and I call 'em what they are." The modern umpire says, "There are balls, and there are strikes, and I call 'em as I see 'em." The postmoderr umpire says, "There are balls, and there are strikes, and they ain't nothing until I call 'em."

Adapted from J. Richard Middleton and Brian J. Walsh, *Truth Is Stranger Than It Used to Be: Biblical Faith in a Postmodern Age* (InterVarsity Press, 1995), 31.

But rather than damaging the Christian faith, Nietzche may have saved the church from itself. He brought to light an underlying weakness of foundational-ism – we had done away with the Unknowable. God, the Great Mystery, is no longer necessary when human beings can know all and be all without him. If science can objectively discover all truth and if, given enough time, humankind can master the cosmos, then where is God in that system? Nowhere. Nietzche's point was that we *killed God*, or, more specifically, *we need God*.

21

It would indeed be terrifying to worship a God we could figure out. The enigmas, mysteries, and antinomies of God are what make him God. Without these, he would be just a very cool guy.

Kara Powell

22

Deconstruction gained momentum in the first half of the 20th century as it became clear that science is not capable of answering all questions and the human mind may not be able to solve every problem. All the foundations constructed during the modern period were questioned, and all of the premises that were taken for granted were scrutinized.

The premise of postmodernism is, then, to question all premises. All assumptions are out the window for a postmodern philosopher, who's on a quest to show that all is relative and nothing can be taken for granted. Skepticism and cynicism rule the day.

Take the presumption that the Bible is the foundation upon which all of Christian theology and practice is built: Of course, that makes perfect sense to Christians — the Bible is God's inspired word, and it's the Christian's rule of life.

The very meaning and mission of deconstruction is to show that things –texts, institutions, traditions, societies, beliefs, and practices of whatever size and sort you need – do not have definable meanings and determinable missions, that they are always more than any mission would impose, that they exceed the boundaries they currently occupy. What is really going on in things, what is really happening, is always to come.

John D. Caputo, *Deconstruction in a Nutshell: A Conversation with Jacques Derrida*, 31

But the advent of modern scientific investigation led to the discipline of literary criticism and deconstruction which, in turn, led to similar practices in biblical studies. Continental biblical scholars at the turn of the twentieth century put the Bible under more exacting scrutiny than anyone had before.

For instance, the modern "search for the historical Jesus" reached a crescendo with Albert Schweitzer, a scientifically trained biblical scholar. In 1906 Schweitzer "discovered" that Jesus was a prophet who had suffered under the misapprehension that the end of the world was imminent. Jesus had thrown himself upon the wheel of history and, though he reversed its course, he was crushed by it. [6]

Schweitzer was not trying to demean the Christian message in his conclusion. He was a faithful believer who was attempting to make the gospel story believable for himself and other educated rationalists. To accomplish this, he had to take the "unbelievable," supernatural elements out of the gospel. His foundationalism (science) forced him into this position. Then his modernism blinded him to the realizations that he was not objective and that one cannot scientifically prove *anything* about Jesus. As a result, Schweitzer's picture of Jesus came out looking a lot like Schweitzer!

Likewise, the Jesus Seminar participants are latter-day modernists working at the same project that Schweitzer and so many others have attempted. They are all doomed to fail, because they are playing with an outdated rulebook.

23

24

The problem with foundationalism is that scientific discoveries and philosophical theories chip away at foundations. In the philosophy of science, for example, Karl Popper questioned the very facts upon which science was based. He said instead of a foundation, the base of scientific knowledge should be thought of as pilings driven into a swamp.[7] So, in the example of Christianity, scholars had to keep propping up the foundation — they had to buttress it, building a substructure to support the Bible.

PRACTICE

THEOLOGY

SCRIPTURE

miracles   scientific"proof"   prophecies

Note well, the problem is *not* with Scripture — the problem is with foundationalism. In a scientifically oriented world, students are going to ask us, "How do we really *know* that the Bible is the word of God?" This is not a question that was asked about the Bible in past centuries — it was a given. Now we try to prove the inerrancy of Scripture, and most often we defend it with a self-referential statement: "Because 2 Timothy 3:16 says it is." That's no proof; that's a circular argument.

But instead of frantically trying to justify our reliance on Scripture using an outdated epistemological scheme, let's stop using the foundationalism of the modern period and get on to looking at Scripture and the world through postmodern eyes — the kind of eyes our students have been born with.

What Is Postmodernism?

The last century has been a time of questioning and deconstruction, especially in the upper echelons of academic philosophy, literary criticism, architecture, and art history. In literary criticism, for example, postmoderns have argued that no text has an actual meaning since each reader imports meaning into the text; even the author's meaning for the text has been deconstructed. Postmodern philosophers have argued that there is no grand metanarrative (an overarching story or common experience that unites all human beings), and they have thereby attempted to deconstruct most philosophies and religions.

25

Western history is now in a time of transition from the modern to an uncertain postmodern period. Indications of a postmodern worldview suggest that mystery, with its emphasis on complexity and ambiguity, community, with its emphasis on the interrelation of all things, and symbolic forms of communication, with an emphasis on the visual, are all central to the new way of thinking.

Robert Webber, *Ancient-Future Faith: Rethinking Evangelicalism for a Postmodern World*, 35

In order to communicate, live, and breathe in this emerging world, it's crucial to get a grip on postmodern cultural patterns and thought processes. The following is an incomplete list of postmodernism's credos.[8]

- *Objectivity is out, subjectivity is in.* One person, or group of people, cannot claim an objective viewpoint. To be objective means one can stand outside of something, look in, and judge it. But you cannot really be objective because you're always standing *somewhere*. Therefore I should preface all my thoughts with the statement: "I am a 32 year-old, fairly affluent, Christian Euro white male living in middle America at the turn of the century," because those facts inherently influence everything I think, do, and say.

- *Question everything.* Nothing escapes deconstruction. There are no thoughts, theories, assumptions, or hypotheses that get a free pass, even if they make perfect sense. By questioning the prevailing assumptions, scientists have made all their progress – it's just that they've too often replaced old assumptions with new ones. Postmoderns are deeply skeptical people.

- *There is no Truth with a capital "T."* Truth is in the eye of the beholder – one person's truth is another person's theory. So, as I found out sitting at a table trying to persuade a postmodern nonbeliever with foundationalist arguments, the language surrounding religion and belief has changed. Everything is relative.

- *Tell stories.* Narrative is becoming the primary means of communicating beliefs. Since propositional logic has fallen on hard times, stories carry more weight in conveying truths. Author and pastor Brian McLaren calls this abductive reasoning. As opposed to deductive or inductive methods, when you tell a story, you abduct listeners from their known worlds into another world.

- *Never make lists!* Things are simply not objectively quantifiable. Remember the scientist in *Jurassic Park*, Dr. Ian Malcolm (Jeff Goldblum)? He's a mathematician who teaches Chaos Theory – everything will eventually happen, and the only thing you can predict is that it *will* happen, not when it will happen. Chaos and inevitability are the rule, so when you make a list or attempt to quantify something, you will surely leave something out (which I surely have), and you will definitely betray your own subjectivity (which I definitely have).

The Spoon

Conceived, written, and directed by brothers Andy and Larry Wachowski, reclusive housepainters-philosophers-theologians-filmmakers, *The Matrix* tells the story of Neo, a messiah figure predestined to save the world from an all-powerful, evil computer. The parallels between Neo and his cohorts and Jesus and his followers are enough to interest most thoughtful Christians.

In *The Matrix*, Neo, the Christ figure, journeys to see a prophetess. In her waiting area, he meets a young boy, "a potential," dressed like a Buddhist monk. The boy is holding a spoon in his hand and bending it, presumably with mental powers. The following repartee takes place:

28

BOY: Do not try to bend the spoon – that's impossible. Instead, only try to realize the truth.

NEO: What truth?

BOY: There is no spoon.

NEO: There is no spoon?

BOY: Then you will see it is not the spoon that bends; it is only yourself.

At that point, Neo bends the spoon slightly by harnessing his thoughts.

At the core of postmodernism is this toying with the idea of what is *really* real: the mind is malleable and easily deceived, and yet I can only determine reality by what comes through my senses and is interpreted by my brain. Thus, the key to understanding is not to denigrate the cognitive, but to admit that perception is reality. All things become matters of faith, and, as Christians, we can become more matter-of-fact about our faith. Having *real* faith in a *real* God is not a matter of absolute proof or absolute knowledge but of belief – of putting faith in God as he has become real to us.

"[Jesus and his words] invade our real world with a reality even more real than it is."

Dallas Willard, *The Divine Conspiracy: Rediscovering Our Hidden Life in God*, viii

Postmodernism and Culture

The Matrix plays with this concept for two hours: what is more real? The real world of rusty spaceships and nasty oatmeal three times a day or the computer-generated fantasy world of gleaming skyscrapers and steak dinners? Cypher, the Judas figure in the film, opts for the fantasy world. In arranging his betrayal, he says,

"You know, I know that this steak doesn't exist. I know when I put it in my mouth, the Matrix is telling my brain that it is juicy and delicious. After nine years, do you know what I've realized?" He takes a big bite. "Ignorance is bliss."

In their rare interviews around the time of the film's release, the Wachowski brothers confessed a love of theology, philosophy, and high-level mathematics. These two men in their early thirties produced a postmodern gospel drama. I recently received an e-mail from Craig Detweiler, who, after we finished seminary, went on to film school and is now a Los Angeles filmmaker. "*The Matrix* is the first truly great film of our generation," Craig wrote. "Lots of people think it's a good action film, but postmoderns *really get it.*"

Those of us who are Gen-Xers are the cusp generation. In college, our parents and the Boomers studied under post-Enlightenment, modern professors. We studied during the transition. But the Millennials are getting full-blown, no-holds-barred postmodern thought. So it should come as no surprise that songwriters, television and movie producers, and advertising executives are embracing the postmodern ethos.

The students with whom we work were born into a culture in transition, and children born today are entering a thoroughly postmodern world. This is not to say that all students will adopt postmodern traits, but postmodernism will be the reigning school of thought, and postmodernity will be the reigning culture when our students arrive at college.

29

It's always dangerous to attempt to categorize a movement while it's still underway, but here's another incomplete, in-progress list of some values of the emerging culture versus the values of the modern/Enlightenment era:

30

w/o respect summarise

Modern Value
knowing

Rational: Descartes epitomizes the modern love of all things cognitive and intellectual. In the decades that followed the Enlightenment, the human brain was considered the apex of the evolutionary chain or God's creation. In either case, centuries of Christian mysticism were left behind in a quest to comprehend God.

Scientific: During the Golden Age of Science, scientists were the high priests of culture, investigating and explaining all things. The belief was that anything, when studied by the human brain, is ultimately understandable. Even God was to be comprehended, not through mystical reflection, but through scientific study.

Unanimity: The vast majority of humans have grown up and lived in self-contained, homogeneous communities — multicultural Corinth was the exception, not the rule. A big deal in a modern American town, for instance, was that a Lutheran girl not date a Presbyterian boy (a Roman Catholic was out of the question). There simply were not many choices, religious or otherwise, in America.

Postmodern Value

Experiential: Strong is our desire to experience, as opposed to simply reading or hearing about things. Obviously, interactive video games are big sellers with middle school and high school students, just as high-adventure vacations are with the post-college crowd. A postmodern with an extra $50 is probably more likely to get a massage or go to a really nice restaurant than to spend it in a way her parents deem more practical.

Spiritual: When we learned how to deliver the Four Spiritual Laws to our peers at college, the first question we were taught to ask was, "Are you interested in spiritual things?" Today, that question is moot – spirituality is in, and religious themes permeate our culture.

Pluralistic: The next thing we were taught to say when delivering the Four Laws was, "God loves you and has a wonderful plan for your life." Today, this statement opens a huge can of worms for the budding evangelist. First, a person may be very spiritual without even believing in God – recently someone told me she has transcended a need for God! Second, you may hear, "What do you mean by 'God'? Jesus, Yahweh, Allah, Buddha, Nature, Sophia, Love…?" Today's religious choices are overwhelming. [9] Modern technology has made everything available to everyone – and its lack of adequate grids of interpretation has created confusion.

Tony's theological shift from modern unanimity to postmodern pluralism may also be applied to race relations. The desire among emerging generations for an authentic lifestyle means being racially inclusive. As youth workers, we understand the need "to go there," both because of our culture and because the gospel mandates it. But "going there" also requires long-suffering, because the pain of American race relations runs deep.

One day I was accused by African American youths of favoritism toward Mexicans. Parents, residents, staff, and young people awaited my response. African Americans wondered if I would neglect young blacks. Latinos — the minorities in that community to the black majority — wondered if I was strong enough to protect their interests when only a few others in my position had.

32

I felt a chill akin to being under the spotlight glare of a televised presidential debate. "Why me?" I wondered. But then I swallowed hard and answered: *That was where God had called me, to both Latinos and African Americans*. I realized I would have to win the trust of the people I wished to serve.

Welcome to postmodern racial pluralism.

Rudy Carrasco

Modern Value

Exclusive: Most people in America agreed that the Judeo-Christian worldview was the ultimate cultural good. Even the TV shows of a half century ago were guided by the moral compass established by Moses and Jesus. (Ever wonder what it would have been like to be the Beaver's youth pastor?)

Postmodern Value

Relative: If the 1970s was the decade of "I'm okay, you're okay," then we're entering the era of "My God's okay, your God's okay." You probably already know that students find Christianity's claim of exclusivity the most difficult to swallow. Instead their natural inclination is that all faiths contain elements of truth and any religion is a perfectly good way to express your spirituality.

Modern Value

Egocentric: Philosophically, the self was highly valued by moderns, and this emphasis reached its cultural climax in the 1970s and '80s when the Baby Boomers became known as the "Me Generation." Building personal wealth and finding sexual fulfillment were paramount, even at the expense of others.

34

Individualistic: With so much emphasis on the self and the person, it's no wonder that modern marketers went after the individual consumer as their highest prize. Descartes did not say, "We think, therefore we are." The individual knower was seen as higher and more pure than a group of knowers.

Functional: Modern architecture emphasized utility — for example, look at the worship center as a replacement for the sanctuary. Ideas and material inventions were to be judged on their ability to serve a purpose.

Industrial: With the beginning of the Industrial Age, which followed closely on the heels of the Enlightenment, human beings became gluttons of the earth's resources. Efficiency and material bounty were the goal. Machines were among the highest of humankind's inventions.

Postmodern Value

Altruistic: Giving away one's time and resources to others is highly valued in the emerging culture, and not just because schools give credit for it. Volunteerism is on the rise, and so are the "helping professions," even as Millennials paradoxically seem to be even more consumeristic than their parents.

When asked why they volunteer to serve others or have chosen careers in the helping professions, Christians and non-Christians alike tend to say that these jobs make them feel "better" or "useful." Ultimately, even our most altruistic acts are flavored with our selfish desires. Maybe that's why Jesus usually promised rewards to those who make sacrifices. It's easier to claim "me last" when Jesus offers the hope that we'll eventually skip to the head of the line.

35

Kara Powell

Communal: For the greater part of the history of humankind, we have been living in community — making decisions with, sharing resources with, and staying committed to others. Postmoderns are returning to community and family, albeit in untraditional ways such as cohousing. TV's *The Real World*, *Road Rules*, *Survivor*, and *Big Brother* exploit this postmodern interest in community.

Creative: The arts are making a rebound and beauty for beauty's sake is highly esteemed. For instance, postmodern architecture seeks beauty interlaced with functionality. Gen-Xers and Yers are known for their aesthetic sensibilities

Environmental: Students are concerned about the planet and its viability in the future. Schemes like colonizing the moon or Mars are losing support (except in movies) — so we are left to figure out how to make it work here. Earth Day has become equivalent to a holiday on many college campuses. The church should lead the way in taking this issue seriously.

Modern Value

Local: Although modern transportation began to form the worldwide economy, most people's interests were still close to home. In the church, we heard from faraway missionaries via snail mail, and the youth group mission trip overseas was virtually unheard of.

36

Compartmentalized/Dichotomized: One of the main reasons the church has suffered through the Baby Boom generation is its proclivity to live in a segmented fashion – the idea that you can be a jerk at the office and unfaithful to your spouse but still be a faithful Christian. The reigning paradigm was the platonic separation of the mind/soul and the body, and what is done in the body does not affect the soul.

Relevant: The clarion call of growing churches over the last few decades has been to preach in ways that make the gospel relevant to people's day-to-day lives. For instance, a seeker-sensitive church decided not to put a cross in the worship center so not to offend newcomers.

Relational: At least one thing remains true: because someone they trust invites them. leaders will always be the best investments

Postmodern Value

Global: In the 1970s, an astronaut in earth orbit declared that, from his perspective, there were no boundaries. He gave voice to the generation being born. With no major wars or economic depressions to unite us, students believe they're citizens of the world, and their loyalties may be stronger to the entire human race than they are to their nations. CNN and the Internet only strengthen this conviction.

We have placed a high value on unity around a mission (e.g., "We seek to transform people through..." et cetera). Youth ministry has been transformed by adopting this motivational, corporate approach. But postmoderns are not unified by mission. They are relationally loyal but tend to be very independent concerning mission. I don't think mission will be unifying for postmoderns.

Brad Cecil

37

Holistic: Postmodern students are deeply suspicious of those living dichotomous lives. The holistic life is one in which every area is touched by every other area. A Christian leader, student, or adult must exhibit integrity in the entirety of life.

Authentic: Related to holism, authenticity is a valued commodity. Some have described this as a shift "from being relevant to being real." Today, the younger generations respond, "Don't tell me how to apply this Bible passage to my life. You don't know anything about my life. Just tell me what it really means. I'll decide how to apply it." That means preaching the *whole* Bible – contradictions, wars, infidelity, everything.

most students (and adults) come to church
Relationships with students and volunteer
we'll make.

Postmodern Culture and the Gospel

Some of these characteristics may sound familiar, for we are already seeing them in our students. The Christian church, however, has not been entirely positive about the changes afoot in culture. Many have written and spoken against the relativistic and pluralistic strains of a movement that denies any objective truth, and these arguments are to be expected.

But we cannot afford to have another cultural watershed pass the church by. And neither can the church become too accommodating of a cultural movement as it did with post-Enlightenment modernism. These ditches on either side of the road must be avoided. In the middle is a road of levelheaded wisdom: being aware of culture and its changing emphases without blindly embracing these characteristics.

38

The kind of Christianity that attracts the new generation of Christians and will speak effectively to a postmodern world is the one that emphasizes primary truths and authentic embodiment. The new generation is more interested in broad strokes than in detail, more attracted to an inclusive view of the faith than an exclusive view, more concerned with unity than diversity, more open to a dynamic, growing faith than to a static, fixed system, and more visual than verbal with a high level of tolerance and ambiguity.

Robert Webber, *Ancient-Future Faith: Rethinking Evangelicalism for a Postmodern World*, 27

Postmodernism is not the evil that some Christian thinkers make it out to be. On the contrary, many postmodern critiques of modernism should be welcomed by the church. No longer are we beholden to the scientific proof model of evangelism — everything does not need to be explained and rationalized. This should come as a relief to Christian youth workers who have been attempting to *explain* great mysteries like the incarnation, the resurrection, and the Lord's Supper.

There is new room in our faith for experience, for mysticism, and for mystery. We can recover *the story* as the great conveyer of truth, and we can use it to great effect just as Jesus did. We can welcome people into a journey instead of getting them to assent to a oversimplified version of the gospel and recite a three-sentence prayer. In other words, we can recover some of our lost heritage. For a long time, Christians have been consumed with maintaining political power, conquering lands, writing laws, and a lot of other things that Jesus did not seem the least bit concerned with. We were sidetracked during the modern era, and postmodernity may afford us the ability to recover some aspects of authentic Christianity.

39

40

Of course we may have been doing the right thing during modernity — it's just that what was once right is now wrong. Times have changed. Makes you think that maybe what we so earnestly advocate today as "postmodernity" may be viewed as wrong in a few years time, too. If this is true then maybe we should talk about our present convictions with more modesty.

Pete Ward

I agree that postmodernity has produced an amazing result — the return of faith. According to David Tracy in *God, the Gift, and Postmodernism*, "That postmodern turn toward the mystics has yielded one of the most surprising developments in contemporary philosophical and theological thought: the amazing return of religion as the most feared other of Enlightenment modernity... The most explosive power in many forms of postmodern thought is the return of the Ultimate repressed by the Enlightenment — the return of religion as a phenomenon demanding new attention, new description, and, of course, new critique."

Brad Cecil

Now that Christians are a minority and those days when Christianity was the guiding force in culture are gone, we can move forward into the future that God has for us. *Youth workers should be looking forward and engaging the emerging culture.*

41

I really appreciate Tony's general optimism about opportunities for being and making disciples in the emerging culture. This is especially true for youth workers. The flip side, though, is that after young adults are given permission to explore their faith in a postmodern matrix — without being required to become "modernly circumcised," so to speak — they'll have to face life in "grown-up" churches which are almost uniformly modern in tone, theology, and structure. So how will they be welcomed by the existing modern church? If they aren't welcomed, I wonder if the subtext of youth ministry for the next few decades will be recruiting tomorrow's church planters. Will we need a new generation of postmodern leaders to plant a new breed of churches for postmodern mission? May God give us both — wise, welcoming leaders who accept postmodern disciples into existing churches and intrepid, innovative church planters who create new space for postmodern mission.

Brian McLaren

42

On the other hand, not everything is rosy in the postmodern landscape. To embrace these forthcoming changes whole-heartedly would be a disservice to the gospel. We *do* claim an exclusive faith, and we do lay claim to the one true God, the one true Savior, and the one true story into which every human being fits. These tenets of our faith will fly in the face of many practicing postmoderns.

For this reason, Christians (and I believe youth workers should lead the way in this) must recover our prophetic voice – not condemn an inevitable societal movement, but stand up to strains and themes that clearly contradict the truths we believe. That is, as culture moves down this wide, new road, we need to be on the lookout for the dark alleys into which people will veer, and we need to shine the bright light of Jesus right down those alleys.

And nowhere do these changes happen faster or get a stronger foothold than in youth culture. Most people in our churches expect us to be the experts on what's happening in the teenage world: that means music, movies, TV, Internet, video games, books, magazines, et cetera. Let's face it, most senior pastors won't watch a couple hours of MTV to see what students are watching. And, sadly, most parents won't, either.

So, as youth workers, we are called to be in a kind of dance with culture – a dance in which we lead and culture follows. To sit out this dance is to lead the monastic life. But the life of a youth worker is one of cultural engagement. Our call is to help our students engage a movie like *The Matrix* – to interpret it and watch it with Christlike sensibilities.

Cultural engagement is crucial, but we must remember that authentic engagement is never condescending. It's not "top down." It's shared knowing marked by equanimity. In the most intimate of dances, there is no leader and no follower. Instead there is a gracious mutuality, a learned sensitivity to the movement, personality, and mood of the other. If we are truly going to incarnate the gospel in this new world, we as Christ-followers would do well to learn the spiritual rhythms of non-Christians and a dance that is, first of all, fully human. As we seek humble engagement instead of power, we will earn the right to draw others into the subtle rhythms of grace.

Sally Morgenthaler

43

Postmodernity may be the greatest thing that's ever happened to youth ministry. The youth culture landscape is becoming much as it was for Paul in Acts 17, and the potential for evangelism is incredible. We have the holy privilege of reintroducing Jesus and the Christian faith to ears and hearts that have never heard the real thing before. But we have to resist clinging to modern methodologies, despite their past — and even current — successes. We must completely rethink what it means to engage and dialogue with teens. Ours are extremely exciting, very promising times.

Dan Kimball

We will make mistakes. We will mention movies that our students' parents have forbidden them to see. And we may be tempted into compromising positions — of this we must beware! But our students are neck-deep in postmodern culture every day, and God has called us to be right there with them.

And if that's true, and if it is true that culture is changing, then our youth ministries had better change, too.

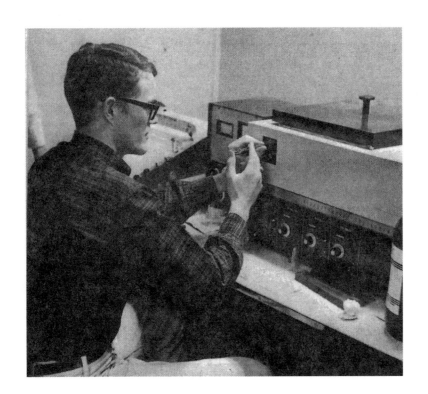

a missional agenda 2

For a long time we've thought of *missions* as leaving our local context and bringing the Good News to another part of the world. That's because Christianity has reigned in the West for almost all of the 2,000 years of its existence. But that's over. The Christian faith no longer reigns supreme. So it's crucial that youth workers shift their focus from caretakers of the status quo to that of missionaries in a foreign land – and that "foreign land" is right in your youth room.

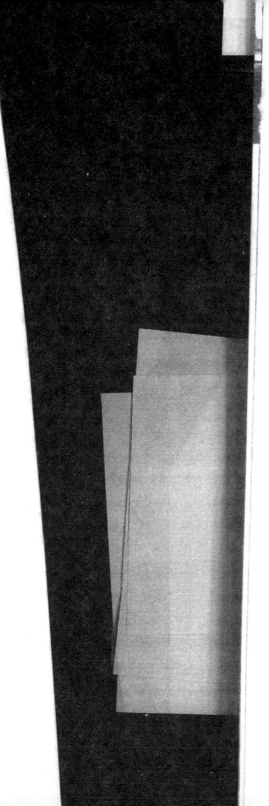

46

Youth workers are missionaries. We've known this in theory for a long time, but in the postmodern world it must be our primary means of self-definition.

Mission work in a post-Christian world takes time, energy, and patience. Youth workers can no longer waltz into a community and think that everyone will come running because there's a concert at church on Friday night. *It's going to be a lengthy process that takes cultural study, prayer, and long-term commitment.*

This is one of the best reasons for youth workers in a town to regularly gather for prayer, fellowship, and discussion. There are other people in your community trying to do the same thing you're trying to do! You may not all agree on the theology of baptism or the polity of the church, but you're all trying to make inroads in a youth culture that's inherently averse to Christianity.

Many times we see ourselves as missionaries, while our congregations see us as program directors par excellence. Then our task

47

becomes helping the congregation reconceive youth ministry as mission.

Kenda Creasy Dean and Ron Foster, *The Godbearing Life: The Art of Soul Tending in Youth Ministry*, 35

As we youth workers begin to see ourselves as missionaries, we can reconfigure our job descriptions so they look more like mission pastors and less like program directors. That means sociological study and forays into the mission field. That means taking a long view of success and being realistic that the culture in which our students are living is working against us.

It also may mean convincing the senior pastor and the church board, too! But if they really think and pray about it, they will hopefully come to understand that we are living in a post-Christian world that's ignorant about the claims of Christianity. And that *youth pastors are really missionaries in a foreign land.*

In Hoc Vince

A.D. 313. Depending on whom you talk to, that year was either the best of times or the worst of times — it was in that year that the Roman Emperor Constantine issued the Edict of Milan, making Christianity an official religion in the Western world.

Christianity had grown in pockets of the empire for three centuries, outpacing the numerous cults that existed then. And due to the exclusivity of the Christian faith — Christians often refused to pay the required annual homage to the emperor — the young church was heavily persecuted. The one empire-wide persecution came at the hands of the Emperor Diocletian, just a few years before Constantine, but the church grew in spite of — some argue *because of* — these persecutions.

Even with this growth, the Christian church was a minor blip on the radar screen of Roman power, as evidenced by the few historical accounts mentioning this newfound religion born in the overrun backwater of Jerusalem. That is, until the battle of the Milvian Bridge in a.d. 312. Constantine — a young and handsome man, reminiscent of Saul, Solomon, and Alexander the Great — was fighting for control of the Empire against his rival Maxentius.

On an October afternoon, Constantine had a vision that many in his army also saw. In the sky above, the Emperor saw a shining cross. Simultaneously, he heard a voice saying, "*In hoc vince* [By this symbol, conquer]." That night, it's said Jesus came to Constantine in a dream and bade him to follow the Christian faith that had been so heavily persecuted over the previous two decades.[10]

Then Constantine did exactly what we tell all our students not to do — he made a deal with God: "If you help me win this battle, I'll serve you and make everyone worship you." In due course Constantine did defeat Maxentius and ascended to the throne, and in 313 he officially enacted a decree of toleration of all religions — the first in world history.

Christianity soon became the *de facto* faith of the Western world. Later, famous leaders such as Charlemagne and John Calvin would even attempt to set up theocracies in which God was the political leader of the state. And it's impossible to walk through a museum in Europe without noticing that biblical stories were artists' most acceptable scenes for many years. One might assume that this God-centered age in which the rulers of every Western nation pledged fealty to Christ would have been a golden age.

48

Approximate years	Period	Characteristics
30-100 A.D.	Primitive Christianity	Apostolic teaching
100-600 A.D.	The Common Era	Classical Christianity formalized in creeds, councils, and the biblical canon
600-1500 A.D.	Medieval Era	Formation of Roman Christianity
1500-1750 A.D.	Reformation	Birth and growth of Protestantism
1750-1980 A.D.	Modern Era	Growth of denominations and mainline liberal Protestantism; Vatican II; American Evangelicalism; Fundamentalism
1980-? A.D.	Postmodern period	?

49

Adapted from Robert Webber, *Ancient-Future Faith: Rethinking Evangelicalism for a Postmodern World*, 13f

Christians feel useless because the church feels useless. And the church feels useless because it keeps on trying to perform Constantinian duties in a world that is no longer Constantinian. So the grace is this: Christians feel useless because they are no longer useful for the wrong thing, namely serving as chaplains in a sponsorial religion.

Rodney Clapp, *A Peculiar People: The Church as Culture in a Post-Christian Society*, 23

But instead of being an era when culture flourished under God's reign, it seems culture flourished *in spite of* God's reign. We could say that the marriage between church and state was less than holy. Crusades, religious wars, abusive missionary tactics, and politically crooked popes, cardinals, and kings were the norm during the 1,650 years that Christianity was officially endorsed by Western culture. (Or was it the church that endorsed Western culture?) While some of Christianity's best theology comes from this period, giants like Augustine of Hippo and Martin Luther and others warned against this marriage of church and culture.

I think all of us struggle, as Tony does, to come to terms with the "marriage" of Western culture and Christianity. On one hand, it's pretty easy to decry crusades, inquisitions, crooked Popes, and indulgences. On the other hand, it's pretty hard to imagine ourselves doing any better if we were in our forefathers' shoes! They had a lot to deal with, you know. (Think about plagues, wars, poor sanitation, illiteracy, and an intolerable lack of good fast food.) In the first few centuries, they had to either ignore Greek and Roman philosophy or else engage it. They decided — rightly, I think — to engage it, even though doing so was dangerous and difficult. Rather than critique them too unsympathetically, I wonder if we can realize how similar our situation is to theirs: we don't have the option of standing outside of culture to practice our faith — our faith can only be practiced inside a culture!

Brian McLaren

51

When the Christian faith was the predominant faith of the Western world, mission was necessarily a cross-cultural endeavor. Christianity was as much a culture as it was a faith, and the church was the most powerful political force on the planet. While theologians had to cast out the occasional heretic, there was no need to evangelize one's neighbors because, in many countries, they were required by law to be Christians, too. But by the end of the Middle Ages, the tide began to turn...

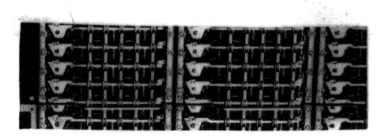

The Copernican Revolution

One of the biggest blunders of the Age of Christendom was the church's reaction to the Copernican Revolution. Nicholas Copernicus and the scientists who followed after him – such as Galileo Galilei – stood on the crest of the wave of science that eventually brought Christendom to its knees. In 1543, Copernicus published *De Revolutionibus*, using scientific methods to show that the earth does not stand at the center of the universe but, in fact, the earth is in orbit around the sun.

52

Copernicus' finding toppled Ptolemy's centuries-old, accepted theory that crystalline spheres explained the nonuniform movement of heavenly bodies. Worse, Copernicus seemed to contradict Psalm 104:19b ("the sun knows when to go down"), Psalm 104:22a ("The sun rises…"), and Psalm 113:3 ("From the rising of the sun to the place where it sets, the name of the LORD is to be praised"). Why would God inspire writing about the rising and setting of the sun if, in fact, the earth is the orbiting body?

A few of Galileo's more fanatical opponents refused even to look through the new instrument [the telescope], asserting that if God had meant man to use such a contrivance in acquiring knowledge, He would have endowed men with telescopic eyes.

Thomas S. Kuhn, *The Copernican Revolution: Planetary Astronomy in the Development of Western Thought*, 226

Thomas Kuhn, a historian of science, uses this example to deconstruct scientific revolutions – also known as paradigm shifts. Scientific methods and theories change, he argues, not along rational, linear, predictable planes, but by random, nonrational, nonlinear processes. Others have argued that other academic disciplines and even culture change similarly. That is, *major changes occur by revolution, not by evolution.* Indeed, the paradigm shift toward cultural postmodernism is just such a radical and unpredictable revolution.

PARADIGM:
An example that serves as pattern or model

But revolution and unpredictability are rarely welcome to those in authority. Kuhn points out how both the Catholic and Protestant churches responded to the discoveries of Copernicus and Galileo: "Protestant leaders like Luther, Calvin, and Melanchthon led in citing Scripture against Copernicus and in urging the repression of Copernicans...[and] once the apparatus of the [Catholic] Inquisition had been unleashed upon Copernicanism it was difficult to recall."[11] Copernicus, Galileo, and other scientists were excommunicated and branded heretics for their "unchristian" discoveries.

53

I wonder if we're ready to consider the possibility — just the possibility, now — that our Protestant-evangelical reaction to Darwin is amazingly similar to the Roman Catholic reaction to Copernicus and Galileo. Isn't it possible that evolution is one of God's coolest designs? Of course, if the theory is even partially true, it requires us to change our interpretation of Scripture and our sense of the universe's lifespan — but aren't these the same kinds of changes Copernicus' new ideas required of the late medieval church?

Brian McLaren

54

We have a reminder of the church's reaction to this paradigm shift in the Campo dei Fiori in Rome. The Campo is known as the most secular square in Rome because it's the only major piazza lacking a church. In Roman times it served as the area for drilling Roman legions. More recently it was the Vatican's spot for executions.

At the center of the Campo stands a bronze statue of Giordano Bruno, the humanist philosopher and mystic who accepted Copernicus' new ideas because they agreed with his own conception of an infinite universe. In 1600 Bruno was burned at the stake by church officials on the Campo. Today his likeness stands there, covered by an immense cloak and hood — his head is bowed, but his eyes are ominously raised toward the Vatican, the center of power that refused to change with the times.

And although Bruno did not repudiate his Christian faith — he was a Dominican priest — on February 17, 2000, the 400th anniversary of his execution, hundreds of Italian atheists, anti-clerics, and free thinkers gathered around the statue to celebrate Bruno as a martyr of their cause.[12]

The Copernican Revolution is one of the more notorious examples of how poorly the church wielded power during its first 16 centuries. It was also the beginning of the end for the church's temporal authority — just four centuries later, science rules the day and the church is clinging to its last remnants of power.

Excursus: Youth Ministry's Ability to React

The example of the Copernican Revolution raises the question: how does the church react to paradigm shifts today? What will happen in our youth ministries when some radical scientific discovery seems to rock the very foundation of our faith?

Here are two hypothetical scenarios to test our readiness for a paradigm shift:

55

- *Scientists find the gene that causes homosexuality.* While Christians hold a wide range of views along the theological spectrum regarding this issue, this finding would rock the Christian world because it would seem to directly contradict the teachings of the Bible — particularly Paul's writings. The first question that students are going to ask is, "So what else in the Bible is bound by time and destined to be overturned by science?"

- *The existence of extraterrestrials is conclusively proven.* Don't laugh too hard — what if it happens? Students will immediately look to us to interpret these events, and we will be the spokespersons for God.

A revolution is for me a special sort of reconstruction of group commitments. But it need not be a large change, nor need it seem revolutionary to those outside a single community, consisting perhaps of fewer than twenty-five people.

Thomas S. Kuhn, *The Structure of Scientific Revolutions*, 181

56

The reason to think about shifts like these is that we need to be prepared. The church has a poor history of changing with the times, and we are living in times that are changing at an astounding rate. The shift toward postmodernism itself is quite dramatic, as is the realization that we are living in a post-Christian world.

Science is no longer the ultimate, but it is still highly valued. To be effective communicators in a culture committed to science, we must be able to speak the language of science. Most importantly, we must give our students the tools to intelligently communicate their faith in this scientific world. And one of the most significant aspects in a scientific vocabulary is the ability to change.

After Constantine

It should shock no one that Christianity's marriage to culture has ended — the Western world has walked out on the church. And although we're living in what might be the most "spiritual" of all times, Christianity is (ironically) at the bottom of the totem pole.

The engagement of the church with modern Western culture has resulted in the marginalization of the Christian faith.

Wilbert R. Shenk, *Write the Vision: The Church Renewed*, 2

In their excellent book on these changing times, *Resident Aliens*, Stanley Hauerwas and William Willimon set the end of Christendom on a Sunday evening in 1963. That was when the Fox Theater in Greenville, South Carolina, had the audacity to open its doors and show a movie on the Lord's Day: "On that night," they write, "Greenville, South Carolina — the last pocket of resistance to secularity in the Western world — served notice that it would no longer be a prop for the church. There would be no more free passes for the church, no more free rides."[13] And on that night, one of the authors slipped out the back door of his youth group and went to the movies.

58

The church exists today as resident aliens, an adventurous colony in a society of unbelie

Stanley Hauerwas and William H. Willimon,
Resident Aliens: Life in the Christian Colony, 49

resident aliens, an adventurous colony in a society of unbelief.

The church exists today as resident aliens, an adventurous colony in a society of unbelie

The church exists today as resident aliens, an adventurous

Of course, they are hyperbolic in their assertion that Greenville, South Carolina, was the last bastion of Christendom – *your* town might be! Obviously, cultural changes do not take place everywhere at once. Most often a kind of trickle-down takes place: change starts in colleges and universities, then moves to urban centers, to the suburbs, and, finally, to rural areas.

59

Given that colleges and universities are the primary sources of cultural change, why do college ministries receive such a small slice of the average church's resource pie? If, in the last century, there were purposeful and communal college ministries offering lifelines to young adults drowning in postmodern confusion, this century would look dramatically different. Instead of scratching our heads and wrestling with how to minister in a postmodern context, we'd already have pinned down some answers.

Kara Powell

60

But it is evident everywhere. Only a few "Blue Laws" remain – those statutes that keep businesses closed on Sunday. City ordinances against sodomy and oral sex, passed by well-intentioned 19th-century Christian legislators, are being overturned. Even the more recent no-homework-on-Wednesday-because-it's-church-night policy at many public schools is being rescinded.

Some may long for the era when everyone put on their "Sunday best" and the vast majority of the American populace was sitting in pews on the Christian Sabbath – when it was a scandal to see someone jogging or mowing the lawn on Sunday morning. Clearly, many were attending services not out of deep faith, but due to obligation – going to church was the only culturally appropriate thing to do on Sunday morning. But at least they were going…

Those days are gone. The Christian faith, for better and for worse, does not guide Western culture anymore. Artists still depict biblical scenes, but these pieces make headlines because they're soaked in urine or splattered with cow dung. The Christian Sabbath looks no different from any other day of the week. "Under God" has been removed from the Pledge of Allegiance in many schools.

Groups do exist that are frantically trying to stop this inevitable slide into perceived rampant secularism. The Center for Reclaiming America has as its mission "to inform the American public and motivate people of faith to defend and implement the biblical principles on which our country was founded."[14]

This mission as stated is dubious on three counts. First of all, it's questionable whether the U.S. was even founded on biblical principles – Christian values mixed with Lockean social theory is closer to the truth. Second, no one in any culture can turn the clock back once the culture has begun to move in a certain direction.

61

When the rate of change inside the company is exceeded by the

rate of change outside the company, th

rate of change outside the company, the end is near

rate of change outside the company,   the end is near

rate of change outside the company, the end is near

Jack Welch, Chairman of GE

And third, we must question whether a "Christian America" is even a good idea. The church's supposed partnership with government was never very successful: the church did not turn out better Christians, and the government was not more Christlike. In fact, the church seems to grow stronger and deeper when persecuted, or at least not officially endorsed. Asian and Latin American countries have witnessed unprecedented growth and revival in recent years, while the church in "Christian" (read: "Western") Europe is on the vine.

The U.S. seems to be somewhere between these two extremes. And we youth workers should hail this change as good for the health of our ministries! As Rodney Clapp has written, we are no longer chaplains of the culture. We need not fear upsetting the powers-that-be who might take away our "place at the table" — we're not even invited to the table anymore![15] We can finally reclaim our prophetic voice, speaking the truth into culture.

And who better to serve as God's prophets in this youth-focused culture than youth pastors?

I tend to agree, although the conclusion is erroneous. *Students* are the missionaries. They're on track with emerging trends. They have their tribes and subcultures decoded. They're the ones learning to translate culture. (Daniel is a great model for that, incidently.) In this pluralistic world, it's too much work for the youth workers to do all the work of evangelism — they must teach students to be missionaries, too.

Mark Driscoll

The Popularity of God

One of the noteworthy characteristics of the postmodern/post-Christian world is the dramatic rise of spirituality. Propositional truth is out and mysticism is in. People are not necessarily put off by a religion that does not "make sense" — they are more concerned with whether a religion can bring them into contact with God.

Polls and surveys indicate that belief in God and the practice of prayer — however they're defined — are at all-time highs. Pollster George Gallup has found that the belief in God runs at 86 percent in the United States. And 71 percent of the population says they never doubt the existence of God — that's up 11 percent since the mid-1980s. God's popularity is on the rise.[16] Gallup also reports that nine of 10 people pray regularly and three of four pray daily.[17]

But involvement in the Christian church is waning — slowly in some places, rapidly in others.

In the article "Teenagers Embrace Religion but Are Not Excited about Christianity," Christian pollster George Barna finds that although middle school and high school students attend church at higher rates than their Baby Boomer parents did, only one teen in three plans on continuing participation in church upon reaching adulthood. Barna concludes that this is "the lowest level of expected participation among teens recorded…in more than a decade. If the projections pan out, this would signal a substantial decline in church attendance occurring before the close of this decade."

It seems teens have a "superficial relationship" with Christianity, in Barna's view. So youths are involved with church at astounding rates — seven in 10 participate in some church-related activity during a typical week — but *fewer than half* of them say church involvement will continue to be a part of their lives down the road.[18]

63

Strange, you could say the opposite for the U.K. Numbers are down, but levels of commitment are up (well sort of). So much for global, cultural change in this new era. Maybe postmodernism is more slippery and less predictable than we think it is.

Pete Ward

64

How can this be happening? The students involved in *our* ministries are telling surveyors that they don't want to stick around church for the long haul. This is a strong indictment against the way we've been doing youth ministry — a mile wide and an inch deep. Our numbers may be up, but the commitment level of church-going teens in America is down.

That's the bad news. The good news is that we now get to proclaim the gospel in a world that *wants* to hear about God. Tony Campolo has said that when he's on a plane and the person sitting next to him asks him what he does, if he feels like talking he'll say he's a sociology professor — but if he doesn't want to talk he responds that he's an evangelist. People are interested in hearing a *sociologist* talk about God and faith, but not an evangelist. People are less excited about following the conventional methods to discover God as opposed to unique and innovative paths to faith.

But while evangelists may never be sought out for plane conversations, people *want* to talk about God, they want to hear about God, and they want to learn of new ways to get to God. *This is a dramatically new environment for youth ministry.*

Postmodernism's Ripples

Because of postmodernism's influence, the dominoes of modern/post-Enlightenment culture and thought have begun falling, but the train of dominoes is still standing in many places. Postmodern thought has deconstructed much of what's being taught in university departments, and it has deeply affected urban life. Much of suburban and rural life, however, are yet to be heavily influenced by this cultural transition.

For this reason, most of the church planters and youth pastors working with postmoderns are in places like Seattle, Houston, San Francisco, and Minneapolis. And that's why a person like Andrew Jones – an itinerant missionary and "Postmodern Apostle" who helps plant churches – moves between large cities. Among other things, Andrew has

started Christian raves – warehouse techno dances in which the music and video moves the participants through the entirety of Scripture, from Genesis to Revelation, between midnight and 6 a.m.

This demonstrates an important feature of this emerging world: the postmodern rock that has been thrown in the cultural pond is causing ever-expanding ripples, but those ripples are going to affect some places earlier than others. You may be in a suburban or rural context in which Christianity still holds sway.

65

66

The number-one postmodern icon is the picture of a blue marble planet hanging in space. One of the definitive features of postmodern culture is its global consciousness. While this global consciousness integrates into postmodern culture differently according to geographic location, very few places have escaped its reach. Anne Hird, in her book *Learning from Cyber-Savvy Students*, shows how today's kids are crossing continents before they're allowed to cross the street. And that's a reality whether the kids are from New York or New Mexico.

Leonard Sweet

For example, in our suburban area, we have a networking lunch for all the youth workers from about five suburbs on the second Thursday of each month. We decided to invite the principal of one of the larger high schools, just so he could meet us, and we could try to establish a rapport. We had no agenda other than to say that we all — both youth pastors and school administrators — care about the welfare of high school students. The principal's response to our invitation was that he would have to get approval for such a meeting from the school board and the superintendent, and that we would have to invite other religions to be represented.

We had no idea a lunch invitation could be so controversial!

As we talk around our network, we know that if we were doing ministry in a small town, we would probably be able to meet with the principal freely and walk on campus (which is forbidden to us). And, ironically, we know youth workers in inner cities who are *asked* to come on campuses and be an obvious presence at high schools. In the suburbs, we're caught in the middle of this cultural transition. In your town, you may be dealing with kids who are postmodern, MTV-watching Goths or with 4-H farm students for whom postmodernism will be a strange slap in the face when they get to college or move to the city for a job.

In any case, one of the strange paradoxes of this pluralistic, postmodern, politically correct time is that the accepted pluralism embraces everyone *except* those who claim exclusivity. So while postmodern people are open to exploration of faith, the exclusivity that evangelical Christians claim will rub up against the deconstructionist ethos of postmodernism. In this way, politically correct pluralism is itself exclusivistic.

67

Isn't that ironic?

The *Visionary's Handbook* by Wacker and Taylor describes nine paradoxes of leadership. The sixth paradox is one that the business world is learning but too many postmodern Christians have yet to comprehend: "To lead from the front, you have to stay inside the story." One of the worst things a Christian can do is to leave her story and start living somebody else's story. That's the fatal flaw of New Age spirituality — it mixes everybody's story into one story, which (ironically) becomes nobody's story. We need to learn the song more than ever: "This is our story, this is our song. Praising our savior all the day long."

Leonard Sweet

A Missionary Mentality

We have to become missionaries to a post-Christian world. It is only by changing our mindset from that of cultural chaplain to that of prophetic missionary that we will be able to forge a new relationship with the emerging culture.[19]

The mission of the Church is not merely an interpretation of history; it is a history-making force. It is that through which God brings history to its goal, and only because this is so does it provide the place where the goal of history can be understood.

Lesslie Newbigin, *The Gospel in a Pluralist Society*, 131

As it stands, Christians have been relegated to the fringes of society. We still perform weddings and funerals for the decision makers who show up at worship on Sunday mornings when it's time to get votes. And the public high schools put up with youth pastors once a year when we gather with our students around the flagpole.

But most of us aren't called in when a student commits suicide or to discuss students' chemical and pornography addictions. School administrators dare not give Christian youth pastors a foot in the door at school. This is a reaction against the long-standing supremacy that Christianity had in a homogeneous culture, and it's not likely to change soon. (Ironically, the founders of the U.S. were adamant about the separation of church and state because they didn't want the *government* to interfere with the church. Today the tables have turned, and the church has been pushed to the fringe of the public square.

Sure, people want strong churches in the community: that increases property values…it keeps kids out of trouble. But the message of the church had better accommodate culture, many think, because we sure don't want a bunch of little Jesuses running around town. Have you ever talked to your students openly and honestly about oral sex? Or, worse yet, really challenged their materialism? The phone calls from parents and the meeting with your senior pastor are almost sure to follow. Better stick to the self-esteem talk again. That's the work of a chaplain.

69

A missionary, on the other hand, comes to her mission field with the express intent of *rocking the boat*. A missionary comes to challenge the reigning paradigms, to teach a new way. A missionary cries into the wilderness of six billion people, "Repent of your old ways! Do not marry the reigning culture! Look upon everything you do with fresh eyes, with a new pair of lenses. Take *nothing* for granted!" A missionary dives into culture headfirst and swims around, learning, perceiving, and discerning.

A missionary prophet does not accept the status quo.

What Tony says here is very important. Postmodern youth ministers can by no means see themselves any longer as simply "youth workers" or "shepherds" to Christian teens at their churches. It's absolutely critical to see ourselves now as full-blown missionaries — just as if we were living in a foreign country. Such is the disparity between the modern and postmodern mindsets. So we must bleed missionary blood. We must dream missionary dreams. We must pray missionary prayers.

Dan Kimball

The *postmodern* missionary cries out, "Question everything!" Postmodern architects, philosophers, poets, and literary critics are crying the same thing in their fields. This is the predominant call of our day.

Learning the Culture

The first task of any conscientious missionary is to learn the culture to which he has been sent. Many of us in youth ministry are fortunate in that we are called to serve God in environments very much like those in which we grew up. (Fortunate, because we already know the language and the values of the students in the community.) Not only that, many of us are closer in age and affinity to the youths with whom we work than to the adults who pay our salaries.

70

Being missional, learning the culture — dare I say it's what Jesus himself did?

You may not agree with Tony's assertion that Christians in this postmodern age must learn the culture of our young people. This may be especially hard to swallow if you take seriously the New Testament dictum to "be in the world but not of it." But perhaps it will help to consider that many Christians in urban ministry believe that credo is essential to understanding the cultures of people inhabiting our cities.

Groups like the Christian Community Development Association (www.ccda.org) promote the concept of "relocation" as critical to effective urban ministry and discipleship. Relocation means living in the community you serve in order to best know its people and their needs. Program hours only go so long, but relocated Christians continue outreach and disciple-making 24-7 by being good neighbors who *are* actually neighbors.

The theological basis of relocation is the fact that, as John Perkins puts it, "Jesus did not commute from heaven every day in a fiery chariot." Jesus didn't just hightail it to heaven for a week's rest whenever things got rough. He lived as one of us, hurt and rejoiced as one of us, and he still identifies with the human race. The book of Hebrews says Jesus can "sympathize with our weaknesses."

Rudy Carrasco

Those of us who minister in places like those in which we grew up start with an advantage: we know the territory. We know how the church works. We know how the high school administrators think. We know what events not to miss (in my town, the high school hockey tournament!) and we know what people value. Because I know these things, doors in my town have opened to me – as a chaplain for the police department, I get to meet kids who would never darken the doors of a church.

Others are called into new contexts.

John Foley is a white guy who grew up in a suburb. For more than a decade John felt called to minister to African American students. Through ups and downs John has followed this calling, working hard to understand the African-American culture of South Minneapolis and to be accepted into the neighborhood.

In the mid-1990s John started the Dinomights hockey ministry, "Bringing Hockey to the 'Hood."[20] Through ice hockey – a culturally appropriate evangelism tool in Minnesota – John gets elementary and middle school students into a tutoring program, into internships, to Christian summer camps, and, most importantly, into church. His ministry to these kids has borne great fruit both in the lives of the players and now in their families. And he does not hide the fact that his hockey team is a place of Christian discipleship, even when he applies for grants from nonsectarian foundations. By being honest about his intentions and by taking his context seriously, John exemplifies postmodern missions.

71

Cultural Investigation

John took the time to learn the culture to which he was called. And he was lucky, because there aren't any "how-to" books on inner-city hockey ministry. That means John could not get lazy and just buy any old curriculum for his group — that's the dangerous trap many of us fall into. It's easy to skip the important work of cultural investigation and instead buy a book or a video series that gives a recipe for youth ministry.

In the 1950s, '60s, and '70s, youth pastors looked to our denominations for guidance: how do we make our kids better Methodists/Catholics/Baptists? In the 1980s and '90s, youth ministry became professionalized, and it seemed that every church was out to hire a youth pastor, at least part-time. Consequently, specialty organizations that catered to youth ministers appeared, such as Youth Specialties and Group. In the late 1990s most of us were looking to a couple megachurches for the recipe: it worked for them, it should work for us…

The problem is, what works in a suburb of Chicago or Los Angeles usually doesn't work here (wherever *here* is) — and neither do most of us have the resources, in finances or personnel, that megachurches have. Further, in a cultural landscape as diverse as ours, there will be no single youth ministry plan of action that will work across the board.

That will be a difficult lesson for youth workers to learn. Let's be honest, we're often looking for the quick fix — what can work for me this Wednesday night? (More than once I've had Youth Specialties overnight me a Talksheets book or two.)

Becoming a student of your particular context, however, means taking the long view. It means committing to stay in youth ministry in a specific locale for five to 10 years instead of 18 months. It means convincing your senior pastor and youth committee that results are to be measured in long-term disciples, not in the number of bodies at an event. It means convincing yourself of that, too.

No curriculum should cross our desks and make it to the youth room without significant tweaking and editing, because the person who wrote it — whether she is a youth pastor or a professional curriculum writer — knows little or nothing about *my* town and *my* students. Anything we use needs to be honed to apply to our students — it needs to meet them where they live.

That's why we can admire Andrew Jones — but most of us shouldn't try to emulate him, because an all-night Christian rave will not fly everywhere. And what Mark Driscoll's Mars Hill Church is doing in Seattle with their all-ages punk/grunge club and their Sk8 church for skateboarders is great — but it may not work in the rural Midwest. In fact, we tried to use one of the songs from *Mars Hill Worship 1*, the album by Mark's church, but in our context it just didn't work.

72

I hope readers will take seriously Tony's warning against trying to emulate innovators. Do you see the irony? When you imitate innovators, you can copy everything but their most important characteristic — bold creativity! On the other hand, if you imitate their creativity, you won't slavishly attempt to copy their "models."

Brian McLaren

Instead of looking at the *means* that John and Andrew and Mark employ, we should be looking at the *ends*. That is, all three of them are out *to share the gospel message in ways that are culturally appropriate.* They have all investigated their particular contexts and brought that knowledge to bear on their delivery of the truth of the gospel. A postmodern world demands that we admit that our contexts influence and shape us — that we be honest about our own subjectivities. And we can use those influences to benefit our communication of the gospel.

Contextualizing the Message

Truth. The word is so slippery in the postmodern world. And you might be thinking just that right now. "Well, if everything's up for grabs, what can we hang on to? Can we at least agree on the authority of Scripture?"

Yes. But agreeing with certainty on the truth of the gospel does not mean that we all are going to apply that truth in the same way. Indeed, we do not even *read* the Bible the same way.

74

Is the gospel some kind of duct tape? "Apply Jesus and he will keep you together"? I suppose when we reduce Jesus to "truth," then we can stick him anywhere we like.

Pete Ward

One of the great insights of postmodern literary criticism is that no one, whether an author or a reader, objectively approaches a text. Each of us is full of presuppositions that color the way we read and what we write. The point of this critique is not that we should quit reading and writing, but that we need to be honest about what *we bring* to a text when we have it in front of us.

The weakness of this whole mass of missiological writing is that while it has sought to explore the problems of contextualization in all the cultures of humankind from China to Peru, it has largely ignored the culture that is the most widespread, powerful, and persuasive among all contemporary cultures — namely, what I have called modern Western culture. Moreover, this neglect is even more serious because it is this culture that, more than almost any other, is proving resistant to the gospel.

Lesslie Newbigin, *Foolishness to the Greeks: The Gospel and Western Culture,* 2-3

For instance, a youth pastor in a rural environment can launch right into Jesus' agricultural parables with little explanation, and the students will keenly understand Jesus' meaning. In the suburbs, it will take a little work to explain the difference between wheat and chaff. And I know of an urban junior high group that went on a retreat into farm land, and several kids thought cows were big dogs! Those students will need lots of elucidation to understand the concept of a "lost sheep."

Even more dramatic is the anecdote about the Bible translators in Alaska who had to use "sea lions" in their translation because the Eskimos had never seen sheep. Were they changing the truth of Scripture? Or were they contextualizing the details of the Bible in order to make its truth accessible to a new people group?

75

A Contextualization Case Study

Have you ever wondered why Paul instructs women in 1 Corinthians 14 and 1 Timothy 2 that they should sit silently in church, always submitting to the men, and yet in Romans 16 he refers to Phoebe as a deacon and Priscilla and Aquila as "coworkers *[sunergó]* in Christ Jesus"? *Sunergó* is the same word Paul uses for Philemon in Philemon 1 and for Clement and some more women in Philippians 4.

Did Paul believe women should be in leadership or not? Both! It depended upon those to whom he was writing. In a place like Corinth, Christians would have been greatly misunderstood and possibly persecuted had they allowed women to assume leadership in the church – it was simply unacceptable in that context.

But in places like Macedonia – where Philippi is located – and Rome, women were more highly regarded members of society. Hence, the baby church there would have stuck out *more* if it *had* suppressed women's rights. Paul adjusted the particulars of his message so as to be a more effective witness to the truth of the gospel in a variety of settings. Thus he wrote –

> Though I am free and belong to no man, I make myself a slave to everyone, to win as many as possible. To the Jews I became like a Jew, to win the Jews. To those under the law I became like one under the law (though I myself am not under the law) so as to win those under the law. To those not having the law I became like one not having the law (though I am not free from God's law but am under Christ's law) so as to win those not having the law. To the weak I became weak, to win the weak. I have become all things to all men, that by all possible means I might save some. I do all this for the sake of the gospel, so that I may share in its blessings. (1 Corinthians 9:19-23)

We can apply this principle to our own work: to the youths we become as youths. And to the suburbanites we become as suburbanites. And to the surfers we become as surfers. And to the Goths we become as Goths…

Trying to be an urban-techno-skater-Goth-suburbanite can be pretty exhausting, if not downright impossible. It seems we have two more realistic options: focus our efforts on becoming fluent in the language of one type of student or gather a diverse team that can speak many languages in multiple contexts. I'd choose the latter any day — sure, it's challenging, but it's more biblical and a whole lot more fun.

Kara Powell

77

A compromised church is a church that has surrendered its mission. The criterion by which we may judge the recovery of the church's identity is whether the church has a restored missional consciousness.

Wilbert R. Shenk, *Write the Vision: The Church Renewed*, 32

That's not to say that we are to compromise ourselves or our standards to communicate the truth of Jesus Christ to students. There is no evidence that Paul compromised himself. But we are to learn the language of our people. And every time we speak, we should be aware of our audience.

Among other things, that means no more hired-gun speakers who travel the country giving the same canned talk to youth group after youth group. Can you imagine Paul, having given his speech on Mars Hill (Acts 17: 16-31), thinking, "Hey, that worked — I think I'll use that one again next week in Corinth and the week after that in Cenchrea"? No. The beauty of Paul's speech on the Areopagus is that he knew his audience, he knew the philosophers and poets they read, and he used that knowledge to shape his presentation of the gospel.

We are the benefactors of Paul's contextualization: because he knew that each church in each city needed to hear a different theme, he wrote all those letters that make up so much of the New Testament!

Your Mission Field

Have you talked to a missionary lately? Next time you get a chance, ask one, "How long did it take you to get established in your community?" Chances are, it was a lot more than the 18 months often quoted as the average stay by a youth worker at a church.

We need to recommit ourselves to applying the principles of long-term missionary work to our youth ministry. Indeed, the people in our church will understand us better if we use missionary language and a missionary mentality. Our call is not to take care of a bunch of already-Christian kids but to save them — no matter where they are on the journey of faith — from a world that wants to steal their faith. Postmodern kids are growing up in a world with infinite options in entertainment, religion, and values.

The answer is not for us to run scared from the evils of the world, and neither is it to unquestioningly accept all that the world has to offer. There is a middle road of discerning, wise engagement with culture. Much as a missionary might wear the native dress of the land in which she is living out of respect for the people, we may take on some of the apparel of our students and their culture. This is not selling out or backsliding. It is a wise, missionary tactic.

79

community

During the modern era, the individual was stressed, lauded, and catered to – sometimes at the cost of the community. But Jesus is not just for *me* – he's also for *us*. In fact, the Bible – from Genesis to Revelation – asserts individual spiritual growth in the context of community. In this postmodern time, youth workers must recover the communal spirit of the Christian faith through worship, a reliance upon the Trinity, and other community-focused and community-based activities.

3

82

I have not given a talk at our senior high group in more than two years. Here's why:

When I went away to a liberal arts college, I found it very difficult to maintain the faith that God had grown in me during junior high and high school. As I lay in bed in my freshman dorm room, crying myself to sleep out of loneliness and lack of Christian friends, never once did I find solace in a funny story, clever anecdote, or gripping metaphor from my youth pastor's arsenal.

I must have heard 500 talks between seventh and 12th grades, counting Wednesdays, Sunday mornings, Sunday nights, retreats, camps, and mission trips — but I could not remember one of them as I was driven to new depths of doubt. Instead I wondered if there was a God, and I tried unsuccessfully to read my Bible or to pray using the **A**doration-**C**onfession-**T**hanksgiving-**S**upplication system. I left high school ill equipped for the university experience. I had never *really* learned how to read the Bible, and I had never *really* learned how to pray, and I never *really* made good, lasting connections with the other students in my youth group.

I was filled with knowledge, but without a community to shape and encourage me, I was lost.

Meanwhile, I became involved with a campus ministry which seemed to sum up faith as an equation of two parts: having a 30-minute quiet time every day and evangelizing one's peers. I failed miserably at both. In fact, I can recall only one student in our campus ministry who really succeeded at these — and he lost his faith two years later on the mission field. The legalistic approach stiffened him until he broke, and in Japan, without a community to help him heal, he stayed broken.

Both of these ministries missed the mark because they valued head knowledge over community.

Building the community should be our highest value — that's the charge Jesus gave to Peter, and that's what we have all inherited: to build the church, the community of believers. Through evangelism, missions, and discipleship, we build the Body of Christ.

The Entertainment Model

Most of us grew up under the old regime. Formulated by groups like Youth for Christ and Young Life, the high school meeting (or club) looks like this:

- 3 fast (possibly non-Christian) songs

- mixer

- 3 medium-speed songs

- skit

- 3 slow songs

- talk

- breakout groups

- prayer from the front

- announcements

83

No one can seriously question that this youth meeting recipe was successful from the 1950s through the 1970s — indeed, thousands upon thousands were introduced to the gospel in meetings that looked just like this. In many places, this model is still used. And in some it still works — because there are still modern students in our youth groups. In this period of cultural transition we'll have to combine old and new to reach all sorts of students.

The problem is, many students have changed…and our methods have not! Kids are devouring *American Pie*, but we're treating them like they're still hungry for *American Graffiti!*

84

In the 1970s and '80s the Sunday night senior high group at our church was the biggest show in town because we had a full-scale rock band with all the bells and whistles. But many of us are *still* trying to nurse that PA system along 20 years later because the cost of equipment has skyrocketed, and we don't know if pouring tons of money into speakers and amps is worth it today. And since our students have seen Dave Matthews and the Bare Naked Ladies 20 times each, our setup pales in comparison.

We're not anti-technology by any means; we've got the digital video camera and the editing equipment, and we try to use them. And we've put together a pretty decent student worship band.

But whereas the band and the videos and the secular music used to be the entry point — supposedly what got kids in the door — now it's a tool for teaching. Technology has always been a means to an end in youth ministry: once it was a means to attract students; now it's a means to feed students and build community.

Our youth ministry has joined the nationwide movement toward student-led worship — and our students love it because it's their own! They design the worship and they lead the worship. Twenty years ago the band was led by adults with some students playing instruments, today it's led by students, and we've got more budding guitar players than we know what to do with. Beyond that, we've got a handful of kids on the tech crew who *love* running the sound board and plugging in cables.

There is nothing particularly postmodern about this — it's just old-fashioned, relational youth ministry, giving students ownership of the ministry. But at the core they are more fulfilled about their roles because they are a part of making worship happen. And what's most fulfilling to them is something they don't really even know they're doing — they're building the community of Christ.

The Bait and Switch

Another possible pitfall of the Entertainment Model, as it has been dubbed, is the double standard. First, our penchant for playing secular music ("Brown-Eyed Girl" and "Wild Thing" were our standbys long ago) is the classic bait and switch. The danger is getting them in the door with the stuff they like (music, videos, et cetera), and then sneaking in Jesus at the end.

85

I can't agree more. And guess what? In the postmodern world, worship is no longer the front door. Relationship — honest, mutual relationship (and usually way outside our worship space) is the new front door.

Gone are the days when we could just advertise an event — when all we needed was a big budget, stage, glitz, and special effects — and hundreds would come. Kids today have literally seen it all. You can be sure that whatever you come up with to "wow" them, they've already been there and done that.

We have to remember that most kids need an authentic relationship with us before they walk through the youth room doors. When they get up the courage to come, it's because they literally want to meet the God they've been sensing in our lives. Amazingly enough, that's what they assume church is about...connecting with God. Tony is right. If we make the mistake of equating technology with a high-impact, spiritual experience — if we forget that technology is simply a tool — we've missed the point entirely.

Concentrate on the "L" of worship...on going vertical (meeting with both the transcendent and imminent God) and horizontal (connecting with each other). Use wires, cameras, computers, projectors, mics, speakers, and other gadgets to help get you there. Just don't mistake the wagon for the destination.

Sally Morgenthaler

86

Some call this the "Storefront Model." Remember those buildings in Old West towns with two- or three-story facades, but inside were just one-room stores? Similarly, many of the bigger U.S. churches used this method to grow in the 1980s and 1990s, both for their youth and adult ministries. The storefront — worship, musical and theatrical events, even advertisements — were attractive. Once the seeker is in the front door, she discovers that the room is a lot smaller and more constricting than it appeared from the outside.

I recently visited a huge youth ministry in another part of the country. The place, centered in a former warehouse, is amazing: a diner, video games, pool and foosball tables, skee ball, air hockey, and basketball. Loud dance music thumps, and movie posters cover the walls. Honestly it's reminiscent in noise, decor, and entertainment of the Original Sports Bar (without the alcohol, of course!) in the Mall of America.

The dissonance occurred during the youth pastor's message to the 500 or so youth in attendance: "Do not be conformed to culture," he preached, "but be transformed by the renewing of your minds!" (Romans 12:2). Then he dropped a sponge in a water-filled bucket titled "The World," saying we should not absorb culture; then he dropped in a rock and said a Christian in the world is like a rock in the water — it might get wet, but nothing gets inside.

Theology should resist the clamor of the religiously interested public for what is currently fashionable and immediately intelligible. It should instead prepare for a future when continuing dechristianization will make Christian authenticity communally possible.

George A. Lindbeck, *The Nature of Doctrine*, 134

authenticity communally possible.

authenticity communally possible.

To a postmodern student, this evening at the youth group might raise some red flags. The whole first hour in the Entertainment Center was rife with cultural influence – and then the students were chided for immersing themselves in secular culture!

We must beware of these kinds of double standards. Students will not respect us if we lure them in with secular music and movie clips, and then a year later in small group they find out that we only want them listening to Christian music and watching *Veggie Tales!* We must be vigilant and look out for those things that might threaten the integrity of our ministries.

I wish Tony had been a little harder on the youth pastor's "sponge versus rock" message. It's cute and simple...and misleading. The analogy (culture is to a person as a water is to a rock) grossly oversimplifies the relationship between people and culture. (Rocks can exist outside of water, but people don't exist outside of culture!) Far better than a facile analogy would be to look at the fascinating story of Daniel, a young person committed to God and yet living in the God-hostile environment of Babylon. (Of course, we shouldn't forget that Jerusalem was sometimes a God-hostile environment, too!)

Brian McLaren

87

The bait and switch is one of the great dangers to youth ministry. The trouble comes only in part by what Tony has suggested. To me, the greater trouble is that students today are among the most spiritual this nation has known — but the modern approach's bait is wrong. Students — and I would suggest adults, too — want the church to deal with the issues that the church should deal with. They want to see religious, spiritual people who are useful in our world. The bait and switch is detrimental because it takes the church away from what it ought be about — "caring for orphans and widows in their distress and keeping oneself from being corrupted by the world."

Doug Pagitt

88

While the seeker service may provide an initial introduction to the church or Christian fellowship, Xers need to be invited into a more intimate community almost immediately. Otherwise they will drift away. We need to establish an effective method of drawing Xers into an intimate community as soon as possible once they express interest in our church or Christian fellowship.

Jimmy Long, *Generating Hope: A Strategy for Reaching the Postmodern Generation*, 156

A Shift toward Authenticity

A serious problem with the bait-and-switch philosophy is its conflict with the postmodern desire for authenticity. Students don't want to be tricked into attending a meeting at someone's house or in a warehouse only to find out later that there's a hidden agenda of saving their souls. Maybe we should tell them up front that we want to save them — at least we'll have their respect!

That's not to say that the Entertainment Model is not appropriate right now in many places. It is, because there are lots of modern churches filled with modern students, and there will be for a long time. But two things must be considered:

First, any model must be carried out with an awareness of the sensibilities of the growing number of postmodern students. Chief among those sensibilities is the value of integrity.

Second, *youth pastors must never become beholden to any model.* Times change, students change, culture changes — currently at an astounding rate — and youth ministry *must* change…not just for the sake of change, but for the sake of kids.

A youth pastor told me this story. Their church had two student worship meetings per week: on Sunday night was the "seeker service," designed for non-Christians, and on Thursday night they held the "believer service" so their Christian students could be fed. One Thursday night this youth pastor was approached by a football player in his group who explained that he had been trying to get three of his teammates to come to church and they finally said yes. The problem was that the football banquet was on Sunday night, so he went ahead and invited them to the believer service.

89

The youth pastor watched with anxiety as these three non-Christians sat with their Christian buddy right in the middle of them. Throughout the worship, the Christian student leaned over and interpreted the service for his friends: "Now we're going to sing some praise songs to Jesus… Now someone is going to tell a story about her faith… Now we're going to hear a message from our youth pastor… Now we're going to pray for our friends who don't know Jesus yet, and I'm going to pray for you guys."

The youth pastor had an epiphany: maybe the seeker service, dreamed up by Baby Boomer youth pastors in the 1970s and '80s, is no longer necessary! That's because one value of the Baby Boom generation was relevance. Boomers thought the church had lost its ability to speak into day-to-day life (sadly, many churches had), so churches were built to look like shopping malls and services were designed to be friendly and nonthreatening — this way people would come in and get the feeling that the church was in touch with their everyday needs. In fact, this is how Willow Creek Community Church started.

90

The trouble with writing about postmoderns is that they don't like to be categorized, explained, observed, limited, reduced, dumbed down, isolated, or put under a microscope. Postmoderns resent our obsession with definition. This generation is longing for relationship, mystery, experience, passion, wonder, creativity, and spontaneity. In other words, they want to go past where the "sidewalk ends." They long for the place just beyond words, the shore of mystery. In other words, they're looking for Jesus. What else do we need to know?

Mike Yaconelli

But postmodern students want *real* more than *relevant*. The church needs to be what it is: a sacred community of persons who follow a mysterious and demanding Lord. When we water down the message of Christ, or when we try to market the church so that it looks like a shopping mall or a university or a counseling center – or when we pretend that we're no different than a hundred other social organizations – we're not being the church. *The church is different. And to be taken seriously, we must be on guard, always measuring our youth ministries in terms of their authenticity and integrity.*

We have a retreat movement in our area run by a consortium of churches. Much of the incredible power of these retreats is the secrecy and mystery surrounding them. The problem is that many people have to lie to the participants to maintain the secrecy! In fact, in every small group, there is a student who has been through the retreat before but is trained to pretend it's his or her first time. Is deceit okay if it benefits the gospel? Of course not! And although this hypocrisy didn't occur to me 15 years ago when I went through the retreat, it does occur to our students today.

Integrity is vital, and so is authenticity. In downtown San Francisco, Seattle, and other cities, Episcopal churches hold a traditional Compline service – all liturgical singing, no spoken words – at 10 p.m. on Sunday nights, and it's packed with young people…the Greek Orthodox and Roman Catholic Churches are gaining converts among the younger generations in surprising numbers…as has been happening for years, a sizable percentage of Wheaton College students annually join a "high church" Episcopal parish near campus, forsaking their evangelical denominations.

Why? These church experiences are *authentic*. Have you ever been to a Greek Orthodox worship service? It's the furthest thing from seeker sensitive! No one is going to mistake an Orthodox sanctuary for a shopping mall or an Orthodox priest for a game-show host. Not unlike Orthodox Jews, Orthodox Christians unabashedly stick out like sore thumbs – they do not fit in, and they do not really care about fitting in.

The Charismatics, Pentecostals, and the Eastern Orthodox church have won. Everybody else should just throw up the white flag. None of them do worship services — they do worship *experiences*. To these believers, worship is not an activity — it's an epic-tivity. It's both timely and timeless. They're experiential, participatory, image-based, and connective — everybody else is rational, passive, word-based, and highly individual.

Leonard Sweet

91

And isn't that what we preach to our youth groups? We tell them we're "only visiting this planet," but the way we talk, and how we dress, and what we drive betrays the fact that we want desperately to blend in. "Don't get ordained," some say, "because kids won't connect with you if you've got 'Rev.' before your name in the church bulletin." That's incredible! We're supposed to hide our calling so that we'll look more worldly to students?! I invited all my students to my ordination and, thanks to my tradition, it was actually *they* (everyone who came) who ordained me!

92

Very true! No longer must we apologize for looking or acting "spiritual" in church. Teenagers crave inclusion in something bigger than themselves — something mystical and transcendent. Many of us still treat the youth room as a game-show set and the church sanctuary as a movie theater — after all, that's what worked for modern youth workers. Seeker-sensitive churches removed crosses and other symbols of the Christian faith from the altars for fear of looking too "religious" and scaring away potential seekers.

But it turns out that what we've been casting off is exactly what young people are looking for — sensory stimuli that provoke a sense of reverence. A body-mind-spirit experience. We must even reassess how our worship space is set up! Is a brightly lit, "cheery" environment the best venue in which to help youths come into contact with the Holy Spirit? Why not consider a darker space where candles evoke a sense of the mystical? How about emphasizing community by focusing the group's attention on each other as opposed to the "stage"?

I believe the paradox — that the more blatantly spiritual our services and the harder we worship God, the more we will see postmodern youths connecting and responding to the gospel.

Dan Kimball

As usual, Jesus said it best: "Enter through the narrow gate. For wide is the gate and broad is the road that leads to destruction, and many enter through it. But small is the gate and narrow the road that leads to life, and only a few find it" (Matthew 7:13-14). Indeed it is a narrow path, and we do a disservice both to Jesus and his gospel when we imply to students that it is anything but the most difficult path that a person can choose. *Being utterly honest is the first step in becoming truly authentic.*

93

The Tyranny of Immanence

IMMANENCE:
The state of existing or remaining within; inherent: believing in
a God immanent in human beings.

The second reason that some churches will appeal to the postmodern generations
is because postmodern churches offer transcendence. *Transcendence is that
attribute of God that reminds us that he is truly beyond our comprehension.*

94

I'll add a third reason for the attractiveness of these churches
to many postmoderns: liturgy offers an alternative to a rationalistic, abstract-belief-system faith. To be a good modern
evangelical meant to have a belief system that could explain
everything. That takes a lot of work — and never works very well
(at least not in my experience).

In a more liturgical setting, I can participate in the Eucharist,
recite the creeds, kneel, make the sign of the cross...physical,
felt actions of the body, not merely abstract intellectual
"movements." In other words, for people weary of trying to
figure everything out, it's more attractive to "behave myself
into believing" than to "reason myself into believing."

Brian McLaren

LITURGY:
the entire ritual for public worship in a church which uses prescribed forms; a formulary
for public prayer or devotion. In the Roman Catholic Church it includes all forms and
services in any language, in any part of the world, for the celebration of Mass.

For instance, many of the older traditional hymns emphasize the transcendence of God (e.g., "Immortal, Invisible, God Only Wise"). Contemporary praise choruses, on the other hand, highlight the immanence, or closeness, of God, like "All in All" which uses the first person pronoun ("I" or "me") 16 times in two verses.

This change in the character of our worship music, and our worship in general, was an appropriate corrective in the 1960s through the 1990s of Protestant worship that had become vacuous and had lost its ability to relate to the people in the pews. Indeed, youth ministry as we know it grew out of this revolution. But the pendulum has swung too far in the direction of familiarity. *The closeness of Jesus to the individual believer has been emphasized at the expense of the majesty of God.*

Meanwhile, science seems to be reaching its limits — while new discoveries are constantly being made, science is no longer the be-all-end-all. Science can answer What? Where? When? and How? but it cannot answer the really big question: *Why?* Astronomy and physics professor Robert Jastrow said this in the 1970s: "Scientists have spent the last several centuries climbing a mountain, and when we got to the summit we found that the theologians had been sitting there for two thousand years!"

And so a show like *X-Files* has startling popularity: in it, science (represented by Special Agent Dana Scully) almost never solves the dilemma. Instead, the paranormal (represented by the now-abducted Special Agent Fox Mulder) rules the day. And unlike most of the hour-long dramatic series we have grown up with, *X-Files* rarely ends with the crisis in the plot truly being resolved.

A lot has been made of the Gen-X characteristic of irresolution or dissonance. For example, take the worship team at our church: the Baby Boomers want to end every song we play on a major chord, a resolution chord. And while the songs written by their peers are often in major keys, the Gen-X songs that we use are often in minor keys — we even have a few that end on a minor seventh chord! (If you're not a musician, that's the kind of chord that makes you feel uncomfortable when it ends a song.)

95

"We can't end on that," the Boomers argue. "It doesn't *feel* right for worship." Behold the modern-Boomer presupposition that everything can be neatly wrapped up and resolved. That's up there with treating the Bible like a propositional, systematic textbook which teaches us how to respond to every situation a human being encounters rather than realizing that it is a conglomeration of many books including poetry, metaphor, and diatribe (some of which seem to contradict the others).

96

This sense of God's greatness, fullness, and mystery is often missing in modern worship. Certainly the course of time

gives place for all kinds of worship moods and attitudes,

for God is an infinitely diverse God. But I am disturbed that the awesomeness of God is repeatedly swallowed up by coziness. Not only the

Church but God himself is dumbed down, made too

small, trivialized.

Marva Dawn, *Reaching Out without Dumbing Down*, 97

To many of us, though, it *does* feel right to end a worship song with an unresolved minor seventh. That's because much in God's universe *is* irreconcilable, unresolvable, contradictory, and mysterious. And much of the popular and Christian music enjoyed by our students' churches is full of irresolution, too.

The Shift toward Transcendence

TRANSCENDENCE:
Being above and independent of the material universe. Used of the Deity.

Currently, many Protestant Christians are recovering the transcendence of God. One of the reasons that Roman Catholic, Eastern Orthodox, and high Episcopalian churches are attractive to the younger generations is that they offer transcendence in worship – they never forsook this attribute of God, while many evangelicals did.

When you walk into an Orthodox sanctuary, you walk into another universe – and this makes sense to the postmodern mind: if there is a God, surely he dwells in a different place and space than we do. God's universe must look, smell, sound, and feel different from what we are used to on a day-to-day basis. Thus a "high church" sanctuary offers "smells and bells" – worship that, when done well, transports the communicant to another realm, a realm where God sits in majesty. This is done not simply through the spoken word, but through incense, music, lighting, architecture, and even kneeling in worship! All the senses are engaged.

A year ago, every youth worker's dream happened at our church: the powers-that-be granted us leave to turn one of the prime rooms in the facility into the Youth Room. As Congregationalists, we come from a "low church" background. That is, we venerate the earthy and the immanent (because our forebears broke away from the excesses of the Church of England).

Contrary to our tradition, however, we have tried to turn our youth room into a place of transcendence. It's amazing what a few $1.99 strings of white Christmas lights can do to a room – with enough of them, you never have to turn on the fluorescent lights! We even installed a disco ball that Julie and I received as a wedding gift. And, although we don't do this for the junior highers, on Sunday nights when our senior high students meet, scented candles surround the room. We want students to feel like they are entering *sacred space* when they walk into the room. At another church students remove their shoes before entering the youth room, and at another they call their space The Sanctuary.

In every case, *students get the strong impression that they are taking part in something unique, sacred, and eternally significant when they come to youth group.* And that correlates with the unique, sacred, and eternal God whom we come to worship

97

Vespers

Vespers:
a. The sixth of the seven canonical hours.
b. A worship service held in the late afternoon or evening in many Western Christian churches.
c. The time of day appointed for this service.
d. Evensong.
e. Middle English: evening star, Latin for evening.

98

At Bethel College in St. Paul, Minnesota, a Sunday night Vespers service has been gaining momentum for more than a decade. It's wildly popular not just among the college students, but also among high school kids. So a few youth workers in our community got together and decided that if the need for regular, corporate worship was so strong among our students, then we should attempt our own version.

I found many Vespers services on the Web, and I discovered this definition on an Orthodox Web site:[21a]

Vespers: Any of the evening services. They follow a basic format:

- the opening Psalm 103 and 104
- the lighting of candles
- a hymn of light
- the evening *Prokeimenon* (the Orthodox equivalent of the Western "Gradual")
- the *Aposticha* (literally *verses on verses* – hymn verses based upon or relating to selected Psalm verses to a given observance)
- Song of Simeon (Luke 2:29-32)
- the *Trisagion* prayers (a sequence of prayers beginning with the prayer "Holy God, Holy Mighty, Holy Immortal…")
- the Lord's Prayer
- the *Apolytikion* (dismissal hymn)
- conclusion

Obviously this had to be adjusted for our own purposes (especially because I had no idea what a Prokeimenon is!). But we kept two things in mind: first, we did not just want to use the name "Vespers" and transform it into an average contemporary Protestant praise and worship service. That lacks integrity, because those traditions from which Vespers comes have safeguarded the tradition for centuries. They deserve our respect, and it is not respectful to steal the name because it's "cool" and "ancient" and then replace the content with our own.

99

Worship, we might say, is where those who don't get paid for it learn and do theology.

Rodney Clapp, *A Peculiar People: The Church as Culture in a Post-Christian Society*, 105

Second, you'll notice there's no space in the order of worship for a talk, sermon, or message of any kind. In order to stay true to the tradition of Vespers, we needed to keep it as a service of prayer and song celebrating the light of Christ which shines in the darkness.

We came up with the following service:

Opening songs of praise (3 songs)

Welcome (from the host youth pastor)

Opening sentence

100

LEADER: *Light and peace in Jesus Christ our Lord.*

STUDENTS: *Thanks be to God.*

The lighting of the candles

Collect for light

LEADER AND STUDENTS: *Almighty God, we give you thanks for surrounding us, as daylight fades, with the brightness of your vesper light; and we implore you of your great mercy that, as you enfold us with the radiance of this light, so you would shine into our hearts the brightness of your Holy Spirit; through Jesus Christ our Lord. Amen.*

Songs of praise (3 songs)

Psalm 31:1-5:

LEADER AND STUDENTS: *In you, O Lord, I have taken refuge;*
let me never be put to shame,
deliver me in your righteousness.
Turn your ear to me,
come quickly to my rescue,
Be my rock of refuge,
a strong fortress to save me.
Since you are my rock and my fortress,
for the sake of your name lead and guide me.

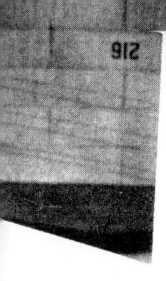

Free me from the trap that is set for me,
for you are my refuge.
Into your hands I commit my spirit;
redeem me, O Lord, the God of truth.

Testimonies of what the Lord has done (students)

Songs of praise (4 songs)

101

Prayers

The Lord's Prayer

LEADERS AND STUDENTS: *Our Father, who art in Heaven,*
Hallowed be Thy name.
Thy kingdom come, Thy will be done,
On earth as it is in heaven.
Give us this day our daily bread,
And forgive us our sins, as we forgive those who sin against us.
And lead us not into temptation,
But deliver us from evil,
For thine is the kingdom, and the power, and the glory forever.
Amen.

Benediction

Closing song

Dismissal

LEADER: *Let us go forth in the name of Christ.*

STUDENTS: *Thanks be to God.*

I totally agree that researching original practice and intent for worship forms is crucial. In our rush to revisit the ancient, let's not forget to do our homework. But just as the the Leonardo Di Caprio/Claire Danes-version of *Romeo and Juliet* radically restaged Shakespeare in late 20th Los Angeles, we can radically reset ancient worship forms into postmodern, artistic expressions and still honor their integrity.

102

Here are a few ideas for putting old and new together in jarring, high-impact ways:

Visually juxtapose technology with the warmth of something "old" — candles in candelabra framing a screen, tapestry draping a speaker, a digital version of Michelangelo's David projected on a screen.

Expand the time frame of your worship band — mix pipe organ sounds and lead guitar sounds, industrial beats with the penny whistle.

Between a praise song's verse and chorus, insert a corporate reading from one of the early church leaders (first through third centuries). Have the band keep playing the song instrumentally (and softly) as people read. Use a digitized, early church icon as background for the words.

Sally Morgenthaler

The service is entirely student-led, and currently we have it once a month with a different church leading every time. We've had Baptist students and Catholic students and everyone in between come to try it out. By no means has it been an overnight success, but it seems to be gaining momentum among our kids.

Beware, this is not a model! This probably won't work in your town – it may not work in ours! This Vespers service is simply an attempt by some youth pastors to meet a felt spiritual need in their students. Stop, look, and listen, and you, too, will sense what your students need spiritually.

Building Community

Our pastor, David Fisher, has a saying: "Individual Christian, the Bible takes no notice of you." While this is strong and somewhat hyperbolic, David's point is that *every* part of Scripture is written to people in community. And, although Scripture has much that applies to the individual, it is always *in the context of community.*

103

We dream of a church where -

_ We listen to and are obedient to God.

_ People who are not Christians become followers of Jesus and pursue a life with God.

_ Those who are not involved in church would become an active part of it.

_ People are deeply connected to God in body, mind, soul, and spirit.

_ Beauty, art, and creativity are valued, used, and understood as coming from the Creator.

_ Culture is met, embraced, and transformed.

_ Joy, fun, and excitement are part of everything.

104

_ The kingdom of God is increased in the real world in real ways.

_ The biblical story of God is the lens through which we look.

_ Biblical Justice, mercy, grace, love and righteousness lead the way.

_ Truth, honesty, and health are a way of life.

_ We value innovation and are willing to take risks in order to bring glory to God.

_ Worship of God is full, vibrant, real, and pleasing to God.

_ Faith, hope, and love are the context for all.

_ The next generation of leadership is built up.

_ Everyone is equipped to do ministry.

_ God s Spirit takes precedence over all structures and systems.

_ Christian community is the attraction to outsiders and the answer to questions of faith.

_ People participate in the kingdom of God in accordance with their gifts.

_ We are connected to and serve the global church.

_ People learn the truth of God and are encouraged to make it central to their lives.

_ Other churches are valued and supported.

_ People's visions and ideas of ministry come to life.

Much has been made of the Baby Boomers' propensity for individualism — hence their other nickname, the "Me Generation" and the era in which they came of age, the 1980s, the "Me Decade." Modern marketing has capitalized on the Boomers' individualism, and, sadly, much of the church has followed suit.

Contrary to this trend, *our primary responsibility is to build Christ-centered community among the students in our ministries.* More than anything else, I feel joy when I see our kids *really* connecting with one another. Those are friendships that will sustain them for years to come.

105

For years interns came to Harambee, the urban ministry I codirect, to learn our "methods," our ways of doing urban ministry and living out our racial reconciliation. But now almost all our interns make the journey to "live out Christian community." Yes, they come to learn from and serve the poor, but they want this experience among the poor to exist within the broader context of "community." In our context, community means physical presence in a neighborhood where one may walk with one's neighbors to key locations such as church, the local ministry, and — most of all — each other's homes. Imagine going to college — to what you would consider an authentic, holistic, really-following-Jesus type of college — and never leaving! That's not what Harambee offers, but that's what our interns (and other seekers) are searching for.

Rudy Carrasco

And, fortunately for us, the Xers and the Millennials are inherently more communitarian than the Boomers. They long for community more than for individually garnered spirituality. Hopefully we can take advantage of this change to move our students and our churches toward an authentically corporate hermeneutic. That is, we can interpret the Bible as a group, as most Christians did until the invention of Gutenberg's printing press in 1452.

Later, under the discussion of creating disciples, some specific methods of doing this will be proposed, but it simply cannot be forgotten that for 1,500 years, the Bible was most often read and heard in community. Could there be a stronger argument for building community in our youth ministries?

A Communitarian God

There might be one argument that is even stronger: our God is a community of Father, Son, and Holy Spirit. At least one prominent theologian has recently argued that the church, and all the ministries therein, should be a reflection of the communal nature of our God. In *After Our Likeness: The Church as the Image of the Trinity*, Miroslav Volf sets out to "counter the tendencies toward individualism in Protestant ecclesiology…[and] to spell out a vision of the church as an image of the triune God."[21]

There has been a well-noted dearth of good Trinitarian theology in youth ministry.[22] Too often, we have focused on the simplicity of the message and left the theology for the adult education pastors. In so doing, we have often lost our focus on the fullness of the Trinity, focusing instead on one of the three persons – on the Father when we teach of God's steadfast love, on the Spirit when we talk about giftedness, and, most often, on the Son when we try to win students to a personal faith.

But God was never meant to be "tri-sected." Instead, he stands as an irreducible and complex "Triunity," as Augustine said – three persons who make up one community. For all eternity, except for about 39 hours between 3 p.m. on the first Good Friday and dawn on Easter, this community has been inseparable, always working in tandem.

106

Trinitarian relations can serve as a model for the institutions of the church because the triune God is present in the church through the Holy Spirit, shaping the church in the image of the Trinity.

Miroslav Volf, *After Our Likeness: The Church as the Image of the Trinity*, 239

Volf's assertion is that the church should be a reflection of the communitarian God whom we worship. And, if you think about it, the church is —

• the covenantal people of God the *Father*,

• the Body of Christ, the *Son,*

• and a community born on Pentecost and constituted by the *Spirit.*

107

When our youth ministries reflect a Trinitarian/communitarian layout, we'll not only tap into the postmodern longing for community in a world filled with divorce and division, but also we'll point with our lives toward a God who is a community and who created us to be in community.

Further, our ministries will be eschatological in nature — that is, we will be a sign of the Kingdom of God which, while partially revealed now, will fully come upon us on the Last Day. Scripture, particularly Revelation, is full of colorful imagery depicting our eternal existence with God. And all of it reveals an eternal existence that will be experienced *in community — in fellowship with God and one another.* So, as our youth groups exhibit Christ-centered fellowship, we point to the consummation of all history when God will gather us in a perfect and eternal community.

While that is true, it's overly optimistic. In the triune community there's absence of sin and a mysterious tandem of equality and submission. That's what the incarnation was — "not of my will, but the will of he who sent me." But in human communities, there's authority and headship because it's necessary to deal with sin in the community.

Mark Driscoll

108

There is a place for Christians in the postmodern world, not as *typically decent human beings but as* unapologetic followers of the Way. There is a place for the church in the postmodern world, not as a sponsorial prop for nation-states but as a community called by the God explicitly named Father, Son, and Holy Spirit.

Rodney Clapp, *A Peculiar People: The Church as Culture in a Post-Christian Society*, 32

There's some good news! We can release that pressure for "numbers," and whether our thrust is small groups, large group, or a combination thereof, our purpose must be to build a group, with God's help, that in some small way reveals heaven on earth…a community that stands out and proclaims a God who exists in community. The challenge will be convincing our senior pastors and youth committees that numbers matter less and kingdom-oriented, holistic communities matter more.

If we define community along racial lines or by age barriers, that's not the community the Bible speaks of. How can churches with affinity groups for attendees with like interests such as "lifestage" be unified and go into the world on Christ's behalf? We're not getting the missiological function of community. And a group of people aren't necessarily a community just because the group is small. Often small groups become a justification for individualism and group desires. And that's just hypermodernity and a new consumerism. All groups in the church — however big or small — should be open and inviting. They should attract and should grow, although the goal is never growth. The goal is health. But if there's health, there will be growth.

Mark Driscoll

109

evangelism

For the last few centuries, evangelism was considered mainly a cognitive process (i.e., Christianity is a set of propositions an individual must intellectually agree with and accept as true.) But more recently, the understanding of conversion has been shifting toward the transformation of the *whole person*. In fact, in the postmodern context, it could be said that we ought to first evangelize experientially and teach the content of the faith later! After all, Jesus says to his disciples, "Follow me!" – not "Do you accept me as your personal Lord and Savior?"

4

Sometimes you just know something's dead wrong. That happened to me once in college. Some of the guys in my fraternity, knowing I was a Christian, told me this story: they were watching TV in the "Tube Room" at the house when two strangers walked in. These two sat down at opposite ends of the room and began a rather loud conversation that went something like this:

112

"Have you heard about Jesus?"

"Yeah, I think that whole Christianity thing is nowhere."

"Oh, really? Well, Jesus says right here in Scripture that 'no one comes to the Father except by me.'"

"So what?"

"Well, if you don't accept him into your heart, you'll end up in hell."

And it went on from there…

Thankfully my fraternity brothers — mostly hockey players — didn't leave these guys looking like the traveler in the Good Samaritan story. But they were angry, and they felt their sacred space had been invaded (yes, the TV room is very sacred to frat boys). And they were more closed off to Christianity than before.

I had a pretty good idea who these guys were, so I sought one of them out. He readily admitted that he had indeed attempted to evangelize my fraternity. I asked if he knew that I had been a brother there for two years, trying to build a Christian witness in the house. He said I obviously hadn't been very effective. When I questioned the efficacy of *his* methods, he responded, "The Lord says, 'My word will not return to me empty'" (Isaiah 55:11).

Now, I didn't know much about interpreting the Old Testament, but I was pretty sure that's not exactly what Isaiah meant. In fact, Isaiah is proclaiming the power of God's word and law even in the face of Israel's sinfulness; it's an indictment against superficially religious people! But I should not have been surprised at this evangelizer's interpretation, for this is just one in a string of modern evangelistic methods that have been aggressive and often ineffective.

A *Very* Brief History of Evangelism

Jesus was the first evangelist, for he took a belief in the one God beyond a Hebrew national ideal, and he clearly broke free of the constrictions that were holding back the religious leaders of his day. His parting words in Matthew's Gospel is a credo for any evangelical Christian: "Therefore go and make disciples of *all* nations, baptizing them in the name of the Father and of the Son and of the Holy Spirit, and teaching them to obey everything I have commanded you" (Matthew 28:19-20a [italics added]).

In the very early days of the church, some innovative and powerful evangelism occurred: Peter on Pentecost (Acts 2:14-41), Stephen and his six fellow deacons (Acts 6:1-7), Philip and the Ethiopian eunuch (Acts 8:26-40), Paul and his jailer (Acts 16:25-34) and on Mars Hill (Acts 17:16-34). Early on, Christians spoke up for God, sometimes quietly, sometimes loudly, and often at the cost of their lives. As we've seen, when the Emperor Constantine became a follower of Christ in A.D. 312, Christianity became the preeminent religion in the Western world.

But the ancient world soon ended and the Dark Ages began around A.D. 500 when Rome and other Christian cities were sacked by Vandals, Goths, and Visigoths. Another 500 years after that, as Western society climbed out of the Dark Ages and into the Medieval period, the church and the state joined forces to stop the encroachment of Islam into traditionally Christian countries. The result was the infamous Crusades.

The cover of Em Griffin's book on relational evangelism, *The Mind Changers*, has a depressingly funny cartoon on the cover: a Crusader sits atop his horse with a huge cross emblazoned on his chest. He holds a spear, the point of which rests right above the chest of an infidel who is lying on his back at the horse's feet. Looking up, the infidel says, "Tell me more about this Christianity of yours. I'm terribly interested."[23]

If Constantine unduly influenced many in the empire to follow Christ because it was the politically correct thing to do, the Crusaders forced many to declare a belief in Christ simply to save their own necks!

As Europe moved out of the Middle Ages and into the Renaissance, Christianity reclaimed its place as *the* religion of the West. Evangelism wasn't much needed until the New World was discovered, and then a *new* form of conversion by sword took place with Native Americans. Through warfare, epidemics, and overuse of resources, the "Christian" invaders of North America managed to reduce the Indian population from between one and three million in 1400 to less than 300,000 in 1900.[24]

113

Modern Evangelism Reconsidered

In the Modern Era, Christianity dropped from its place of prominence and was usurped by science. Christians valiantly sought to proclaim the truth of the gospel in a world that seemed to be slipping away. New and innovative methods have been tried: videos hung on doorknobs and television crusades replaced tent revivals. But the results have remained the same: some are won for Christ, but our newer, more "effective" methods are not greatly increasing the size of the church. That's why Milton Rudnick, in his history of evangelism writes, "Although people are won for Christ by deliberate, carefully-planned evangelism efforts, the number is not large."[25]

Clearly the problem is not with the content of the gospel, it's with our methods. If the gospel is a painting, we've put it in the wrong frame. This is not to judge or demean any evangelist or youth pastor — we didn't even realize we had become complicit with culture in the ways we shared the message. With the best of intentions, we've been unwittingly beholden to the modern, rationalistic mindset when attempting to influence students to follow Christ.

Jesus spoke Aramaic. That is, even Jesus contextualized his message — he spoke the same language his friends spoke. So it's not that we've got to go around speaking Greek and Hebrew to students so they'll understand the gospel. But Jesus did question the common pre-suppositions — religious, political, and social — of his day *because the gospel demanded it.*

While no cultural movement is more right or more wrong, it seems the individualistic, scientific approach of modernism was quite antithetical to Christianity. And while postmodernism contains some serious evangelistic challenges such as relativism, pluralism, and the "death of truth," we must respectfully disagree with popular Christian thinkers who proclaim that postmodern thought is dangerous and will be short-lived.

Instead, these postmodern days can be seen as a uniquely promising time for the spread of the gospel. As more and more postmodern students enter our ministries, we will have great opportunities to take advantage of: people are open to religion and faith. God has reached a place of prominence in popular film, TV, and music. Students are looking to discover their own "truth" — and we have truth to offer!

114

115

If you compare world history to a game of Jenga, you'd see that the church let modernity lay down the bottom blocks — and they're labeled *rationalism, empiricism, consumerism,* and *individualism.* That's why it's so hard for the church to embrace the idea that postmoderns don't accept modernity's foundational principles. The modern church is stuck on nostalgia — and it may very well have lost its first love. God's glory might be welcome in the church, but whether or not God's authority is welcome is highly debatable. Anytime we preach a gospel of felt needs and self-esteem instead of a gospel of repentance — anytime we help Christians to actualize their potential rather than to be humble worshipers — we've stopped preaching the gospel.

Mark Driscoll

Extra Ecclesiam Nulla Salus

The church's understanding of itself, the gospel, and the world is always reflected in the content and manner of its evangelization. The church that is not evangelizing is a church that does not truly believe the gospel. It is a faithless church.

Wilbert R. Shenk, *Write the Vision: The Church Renewed*, 54

116

In the last few decades, some youth pastors have outsourced evangelism. We have divorced evangelism from the church and given it away to parachurch organizations and stand-alone evangelists. It wasn't meant to be this way!

Maybe it was because those of us who work for churches have lost our knack for evangelism, or maybe we've run into too many headaches from our committees and senior pastors (fun programs are sure to bring in more kids than evangelistic messages). Or maybe it's just been easier to bring the kids downtown to the big arena to hear a well-known speaker fire up 10,000 students and have an altar call with thousands coming forward than it is to do the long, hard work of tending the souls of those students who do not yet know Jesus.

In the middle of the 20th century, parachurch outreach ministries like Youth for Christ and Young Life blossomed because the church shirked its duty. In some ways, the boom of professional, church-based youth ministry grew as an embarrassed reaction to the success of those ministries. Is it heresy to say that if the church were doing its job Youth for Christ and Young Life would be put out of business?

Tony enters the church-parachurch fray by saying that parachurch ministries thrived because the churches had shirked their duties. That's probably true. But I can also imagine concerned Christians, discipled effectively by their churches, banding together to do cooperative outreach to high schools, colleges, prisons, and other special populations...and voilà, you have parachurch organizations that exist precisely because the churches were doing their duty!

Brian McLaren

117

In the early church, there was an important theological doctrine: *extra ecclesiam nulla salus* – there is no salvation outside of the church. Since the church is, in Paul's words, the "Body of Christ" (Romans 12:5; 1 Corinthians 12:12), the thinking was that one must be matriculated into the church in order to be saved. This is not a legalistic, you-must-partake-of-the-sacraments-in-order-to-be-saved doctrine, but an acknowledgment that when Jesus gave Peter the keys of the church (Matthew 16:18-19), he bestowed upon the church the power to act as his surrogate on earth. Just a few weeks later, Jesus sent the Holy Spirit at Pentecost to empower the church in this task.

Salvation

Salvation and the church cannot be separated.

Salvation and the church cannot be separated.

Miroslav Volf, *After Our Likeness: The Church as the Image of the Trinity*, 174

If we are honest, we all can probably look back at some of those big, rally-type events with the well-known speaker from out of town, watching a bunch of kids go forward at the altar call and "become Christians." But I look back now and wonder if those students really knew what they were doing. Will those students stand before God and be held accountable one way or another for that decision? Or will *we* be held accountable for leading kids down a primrose path?

118

We are working with students who are bombarded with the message of Jesus at rallies, on TV, by us and their parents, and at church on Sunday morning – and it's almost exclusively *with words*. Instead, *let's invite kids **into** the Body of Christ, **into** a community that lives out the moral imperatives of Scripture.* In that way, we'll be evangelizing postmodern kids in a postmodern way. Just as the Word became flesh and dwelt among us, our youth groups – as Christ's Body – must "flesh out" the gospel message.

Many of us have told students that it doesn't matter if you go to church or not to be saved, it only matters if you've accepted Jesus into your heart. In fact, salvation is a lot more complex than that – it's more of a process, more mysterious and less definable than we might think.

It's not that hard to define what youth ministry should look like in the future (which is now). No words. No programs. Future ministry should be characterized by silence, solitude, worship, reading, praying, listening, paying attention, and being.

Mike Yaconelli

Where Is He Knocking?

It may come as a revelation to us when we discover that when Christ says, "Here I am! I stand at the door and knock," (Revelation 3:20a) he is talking about knocking on the door of the *church!* I used to think he was knocking at the door of *my heart.* Turns out that whole section about spitting out the lukewarm and knocking at the door is written to a church, not to individuals. Indeed, some of our favorite catch phrases – "inviting Jesus into *my heart*" and accepting him as "*my* personal Lord and Savior" – are not even biblical phrases.

Romans 10: 8-10 does emphasize the individual, intellectual conversion that has dominated Christian youth ministry: "if you confess with your mouth, 'Jesus is Lord,' and believe in your heart that God raised him from the dead, you will be saved," and the personal decision *is* an aspect of Christian salvation. But many of us have also changed "For God so loved the world that he gave his only son" to "For God so loved *Jimmy* that he gave his only son," and in doing so we have *changed* Scripture's intent.

Salvation is a complex process that involves the individual and the community and results in a disciple who bears fruit. If we oversimplify that process, assuming that's the only way that students will understand it, we're selling them short!

There will always be exceptions, like the thief on the cross, but the clear desire of Jesus and the Apostles was that individuals work out their faith in the context of *community.*

119

Tony's words hold a lot of merit — but we do have clear examples of the salvation of the individual in Scripture (e.g., Philip and the Ethiopian in Acts 8; Jesus and the woman at the well in John 4). And I believe that salvation is based on the individual's decision, not the community's. Revelation 20:15 states, "if *anyone's* name was not found written in the book of life..." not "if *a community's* name." But while we're each accountable to God individually, our faith must be lived out and shared in the context of community. After all, what was the woman at the well's first act after meeting Jesus? She ran off, leaving her pitcher behind, and told those in her community about him.

Dan Kimball

120

The modern sensibility says the individual knower is the ultimate. Thus, modern evangelistic methods were aimed at the individual conversion – accepting Jesus into *my* heart. The strength of this modern emphasis is the responsibility of the individual believer for her own faith and salvation. Blending into the crowd and being one amid the masses was no longer acceptable – and the idea of individual accountability before God on the Last Day was recovered. Individualism was furthered with the invention of the printing press in the late 15th century. The Bible was put in people's hands in a language they could read, and from this came a greatly increased knowledge of faith, theology and biblical literacy. No longer was the truth of Scripture mediated by the church. All of these emphases were positive correctives after centuries of authoritarian rule.

But with all of this individual knowledge and the concurrent social theory about individual rights and freedoms (e.g., the U.S. Constitution) came an emphasis on individual conversion at the expense of the Christian community. Rarely were individuals who converted to Christianity encouraged to become committed church members – the thought was, "They're going to heaven, their souls are saved, if they decide to go to church, it's a bonus." So "closing the deal" was paramount; follow-up was rarely valued.

This has led Wilbert Shenk to write, "The conjunction of Enlightenment anthropology and revival preaching that emphasized the *individual* – without relating this to society/church – undermined the meaning of church."[26] In other words, modern evangelistic methodology, particularly seen in youth evangelism, actually worked *against* the development of Christ's body on earth because soul-winning was stressed over disciple-making. The two cannot be separated.

In youth ministry, this individualistic trend shows itself in our emphasis on numbers. Several movements have been promulgated in recent years that push the goal of every high school student in America hearing the gospel by 2000 or 2001 or… (the year seems to keep moving back). For one thing, this is based on a misguided idea that Jesus will return when everyone on the planet has heard his name – as if Jesus' return is contingent upon human action.

When it comes to postmodern evangelism, I have more questions than answers. So I have decided to go to the source itself: our students. When I ask students from non-Christian homes what brought them into relationships with Jesus, the top responses involve community. Whether they're invited to youth group by a believing friend, or stumbling into Christian community on their own, most students I ask confirm Tony's proposition that relationships with others serve as a precursor to a relationship with God.

Kara Powell

And further, hearing Jesus' name at an altar call or on a beach does not a disciple make. Dallas Willard says the invitation to follow Christ has become so familiar that "People think they have heard the invitation. They think they have accepted it – or rejected it. But they have not."[27] Christianity's marriage to Western culture in modern times has resulted in an over familiarity with the gospel, especially in North America. It seems that everyone has heard the invitation on TV or the radio or a street corner. We've used the machine-gun approach instead of the rifle approach.

Two examples of this: A man who discipled me in college said that some evangelists are called to sit in an apple orchard and wait for the fruit to ripen so it could be harvested. His own self-professed calling was to move quickly from orchard to orchard, plucking the fruit that was ripe and leaving the rest behind. That's called rationalization by a numbers-hungry evangelist.

The Apostle Paul did not pretend that he was taking a survey.

The Apostle Paul did not pretend that he was taking a surve

Em Griffin, *The Mind Changers*, 34

Once, as a part of an evangelism conference, I went to a shopping mall and shared the *Four Spiritual Laws* with strangers. One man — I can still remember his face — decided it made sense, and he said the prescribed prayer of salvation on the back page. There was a place on the back of the *Four Laws* booklet to write the name and phone number of a church in the area for him. But I didn't know any churches near the mall, so I left it blank. I have always felt guilty about that. And I felt even guiltier when we went back to the conference and the delegate from my group got up to announce how many people had accepted Christ because of our efforts. Was that man *saved* that day because he said a prayer? Did he ever find a church? Will I see him in heaven?

122

> **Tony tells a story that is true for many of us: Using the Four Spiritual Laws, we lead complete strangers to Christ...then have no place to send them. He felt guilty about contributing to the spiritual orphanage — and so did I, and so did you. In urban ministry, we call this the "gospel playboy" approach. The gospel playboy makes spiritual babies but then abandons them, leaving them spiritually orphaned. Just as real-life playboys leave children fatherless, gospel playboys also hurt new believers when they fail to connect them to the Body of Christ.**
>
> **Rudy Carrasco**

While Romans 10:8-10 can be cited to support this kind of say-the-sinner's-prayer evangelism, then what do you do with John 6:53-56 in which Jesus states that one must drink his blood to know him? Or with 1 Peter 3:21 which implies that baptism saves? These verses give credence to the Roman Catholic sacramental view of salvation. All this to say, *to become too parochial or narrow-minded in our understanding of salvation is anti-biblical.*

I think I led that man down the wrong path that day. Not because I shared with him how much Christ loves him, but because my words and my actions implied that he could do it alone, that his soul was in good shape because he said a 15-second prayer. My very actions undermined the communal nature of the Christian message.

Our students need to hear that they *cannot* do it alone. For example, no one can be a Christian middle school student without the support of other Christians. For it is impossible to live out the imperatives of the Christian life outside of the Christian community.

The Curse of Efficiency

In our quest for numbers, we have also been driven to chase the bane of modern, industrial society: efficiency. We want to be *effective* evangelists, to share the message with as many students as possible as well as we possibly can. That's a good thing. But *effectiveness* quickly gets transformed into *efficiency*.

Jesus: "I don't like crowds"

123

Me: "You don't like crowds?!? What are you talking about?!"

Jesus: "I don't like crowds. Go back and read my story. Yes, I had crowds from time to time, but most of the people in them just wanted more wine, food, and power. Then — when I didn't give them what they wanted — they killed me. Nope. I don't like crowds. Besides, my best work was done one on one. You know the woman at the well, the crazy guy, the blind man, the prostitute. That's when I did my best stuff."

Me: "But...um...that isn't very efficient."

Jesus: "I know. I don't believe in efficiency."

Me: "What?!?"

Jesus: "Let me put it this way. I believe in making disciples one at a time. Very slow stuff."

Mike Yaconelli, *Youthworker* (January/February, 2000), 72

124

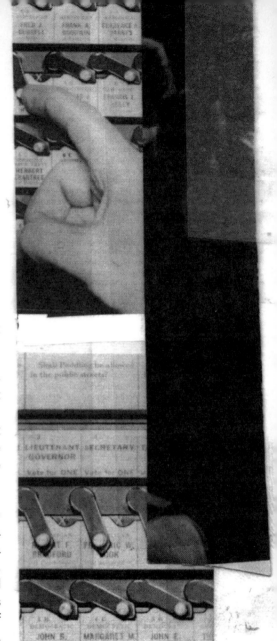

The desire of any good modern mind is to be efficient – to build a better machine, to refine the process, to work the kinks out of the system. Henry Ford is the paragon of modern-systems thinking for refining the assembly line process until it was squeaky clean. To achieve this, he not only got his workers to do one thing over and over the same way and have those various things done in the correct order, he also got each of those workers to do their own, individual tasks with the least possible waste of time and motion.

This desire to remove anything extraneous from the system is called *reductionism*, and it is reminiscent of and related to Descartes' foundationalism. In theory, companies can get more productivity out of laborers who waste no resources, personal or otherwise, while completing their tasks.

In modern youth ministry, reductionism showed in our proclivity to purchase a program or curriculum, or take our kids to a really hyped-up rally rather than do the long, hard work of building relationships and sharing Christ over time. Let's face it, it's often easier to pass off the work of evangelism to someone who has a "gift" for it, someone who's a really dynamic speaker, than to do it ourselves.

While not minimizing the importance of spiritual gifts, Tony's right that most (some would say all) of them are part of a fruitful Christian life. Just as those who lack the gifts of giving or mercy have no excuse to be stingy or mean, those without the gift of evangelism have no excuse to keep the gospel to themselves. Instead, youth workers who know they lack expertise in evangelism must seek mentoring from colleagues, teammates — and yes, even students — who have it.

Kara Powell

125

Further, most of our senior pastors were trained in modernistic seminaries and churches, and they thrive on effectiveness, efficiency, and *numbers*. So we look for the most effective and efficient way to get the message of Christ into the ears of the largest number of kids. So we run a huge camp or a big New Year's Eve party or host a concert by a Christian band or an evangelist.

And as youth pastors, we're caught in a bind: *lots of kids make "decisions" at camps or events, and that goes in the annual report, and your annual report looks good to the youth committee because it looks good to the elder board because it makes the church look good to the denominational office, so the youth ministry is rewarded with a bigger budget and maybe another paid staff member or a half-time secretary so that you can get out there and get more kids to make decisions!*

But then you lie awake in bed at night and wonder, "How am I ever going to follow up with all of these kids who made decisions last summer? And were their decisions even real? Did they know what they were deciding?" And you start working harder and working more hours and staying home less to follow up with all the kids who've made decisions, and you never see your friends or your family because you're always with kids. All because you got efficient.

126

We've missed the point! Yes, we've heard a hundred times that Jesus spent the vast majority of his time with 12 guys, but that's a cliché that does little to take the heat off when your senior pastor is wondering why your Sunday night group still numbers only 12 kids!

In the modern church, "The key problem to be solved was to find the right methods and techniques and to organize a campaign, crusade, or drive. This put a premium on program rather than the formation of a community of disciples."[28] We've taken salvation, a complex concept that Jesus spent his life living out and teaching and that theologians have been trying to explain for 2,000 years, and we've reduced it to Four Laws and a quick prayer. Does that really do justice to the message *Jesus* died to share?

It's up to youth workers to help turn the tide — and we can change the course of American church history! It will mean standing up to our committees and senior pastors and saying we're about building a community of disciples rather than running huge programs with tons of kids.

Some of us might even get fired for this kind of stance — it's going to be risky. We're going to have to find our prophetic voice and say there's a whole new way of evangelizing students.

When you strip away power from those who have power over you, you risk threatening the power structure. When you refuse to measure, you anger the measurers. When you knock the props out of the institution, the institution will eliminate you as quickly as it can. The gospel has *always* been counter-cultural. It was counter-cultural 2,000 years ago. It was counter-cultural 500 years ago. And 100 years ago and 50 years ago and today. Genuine youth ministry always causes trouble.

Mike Yaconelli

"I Think, Therefore I'm Saved"

The first time I went out to "share my faith" door-to-door at college, I got a strange feeling. How could I presume to take all the biggest questions of life — the questions that these students had committed four years of their lives and tens of thousands of their parents' dollars to answer — waltz into their dorm rooms, and answer them in 15 minutes? The reason I was given is that some of the greatest Christian minds of our century had gotten together and honed the Christian gospel into these four propositions.

But why didn't God just give us a systematic theology book instead of a book of stories, poems, and letters? Why did God gift us with 10,000 years of Jewish and Christian history — and many of the greatest minds ever born trying to examine it all — if he just wants us to simplify his steadfast love for us into a list of propositions?

127

PROPOSITIONAL:
Containing only logical constants and having a fixed truth-value.

To treat evangelism simply as the proclamation of an "objectively true" gospel is to do serious violence to the New Testament concept about the proclamation of Christ—not propositions about Christ, but the full person and work of Christ himself.

Alister McGrath, *A Passion for Truth: The Intellectual Coherence of Evangelicalism*, 178

128

These are obviously rhetorical questions. The fact is, the church in general and student ministry specifically have fallen into the modern trap of the cognitive. In the world that has blossomed since the Enlightenment, the human mind has been understood as the pinnacle of creation, and so to win over the mind is the highest good for any conceptual scheme. In the view of the church, if an individual intellectually assents to John 3:16 or some other proposition-al statement of the gospel, then that person has been won. Where the mind leads, the body and the spirit will surely follow, the argument goes.

Why, then, do we run into so many students (and adults) who have said the sinner's prayer and answer "yes" to polls that ask, "Do you believe that Jesus Christ is the Son of God?" – and yet their lives in no way reflect that belief?

Many of our students recently went south to Cancun, Mexico, for spring break – these are kids who profess a great love for Christ, attend youth group every week, counsel younger kids at camps and retreat, and wear WWJD bracelets. Yet many of them spent the week in Mexico binge drinking, entering wet T-shirt contests, and going back to hotel rooms with someone they just met on the dance floor.

It should not surprise us when non-Christians act like non-Christians – they don't know Jesus, and they should not be held to the standards to which Christians are held. What *is* shocking is when people who *do* know Jesus so brazenly act as though they don't – when that church elder shows up with a $10,000 mink coat on Sunday, when the deacon leaves his wife, or when the most solid kid you've got goes to a party and gets a girl he just met pregnant.

Meghan

Meghan started coming to our church just a few months ago. Sitting in our small group for seniors one Sunday night, I saw tears welling up in her eyes. We were studying Ephesians, and we were discussing Paul's thoughts on what it takes to follow Christ. "If you're really a disciple," someone said, "you *will* be considered a freak by most people – even by most people who think they are good Christians."

When I saw the tears in Meghan's eyes, I asked her what was wrong. "I've been to every youth group in town," she replied. "Why hasn't anyone ever told me this before?"

Because everyone had been doing youth ministry with modern presuppositions, and what mattered was that they had won Meghan's *mind*. She had assented to the propositions, she had said the sinner's prayer, and so she was one of the Christian kids.

But one night, Meghan's boyfriend, Dan – the kind of Christian kid who puts my feeble faith to shame – went to her house and said, "Meghan, you say you believe all this stuff, but I don't see anything in your life to show it."

That was it. The end. Meghan had been ruined for the life of this world. She quit drinking, her friends dumped her, and now she and Dan are living out their senior year at church and with each other on the weekends because no one calls them.

129

Meghan stopped by my office today to tell me about the trip to Cancun. She told me about how much grief she and Dan took for not drinking, about her friends drinking until they puked, about kids dancing half-naked in clubs. And she told me about her 18-year-old friend who "hooked up" with a 24-year-old guy, "I hated it," Meghan said, "But a year ago, it would have been the greatest week of my life."

Meghan has been ruined for that kind of darkness. Even though the pain and fear of this new life of discipleship brings tears to her eyes, she says she would not go back for anything. She has discovered what it means to go beyond mere intellectual assent to a holistic life, lived entirely for Christ. The propositions to which she had assented many times before never came to life for her – Jesus became real when she experienced him in a community that loves her with Jesus' love. Finally the Bible made sense to her! Finally she had the fortitude to live her life for Jesus.

You see, Jesus does not offer Meghan a set of propositions. He does not have a theological treatise at the ready when someone crosses his path. He offers life. He offers a transforming and accepting community of faith. He offers truth – truth that comes to life in community. When asked what must be done to live within this new kingdom he was establishing, Jesus did not pull out a doctrinal statement and ask his followers to sign at the bottom. He simply – and profoundly – said, *"Come, follow me."*

The Church thus does not claim to possess

absolute truth: it claims to know where to point for guidance (both in thought and action) for the common search for truth.

130

Lesslie Newbigin, *The Gospel in a Pluralist Society*, 168

We have done a disservice to Christ's gospel by making it into tracts and statements of faith. While these methods of evangelism have made many converts, have they made many *disciples*? The gospel is something to be accepted with our minds, but it is so much more!

If Meghan is any example of a postmodern student, she was won to radical discipleship not by intellectual assent but by the example of a friend, by a loving and accepting community, and, ultimately, by the steadfast love of God.

"I Cry, Therefore I'm Saved"

It's the end of a long week of camp, everyone's sad about leaving tomorrow, everyone's physically and emotionally exhausted, and it's time for the last chapel service of the week. The speaker gets up and really lays on a great talk about the cross and Jesus' death, the band softly plays "Friends Are Friends Forever" in the background, and hysterically crying campers come forward one after the other to give their miserable, sinful selves over to Christ.

Em Griffin makes no bones about this style of evangelism: he calls it emotional rape.

131

> The average preadolescent is not equipped to withstand the positive incentive of counselor approval or the negative force of group condemnation. The phrase "age of consent" in our legal code points to the fact that children may be unable to say no to the forceful persuader. Jesus made it clear that leading a child astray is a particularly heinous act. I think this applies to the methods used as well as the intended results.[29]

This kind of talk on the last night of camp is how I decided to follow Christ, and it is a method many of us have used in our ministries.

But one night I was at a winter retreat with a bunch of junior highers and the speaker gave the bloodiest Jesus talk I'd ever heard. First he talked about a Russian woman who was trapped under a building after an earthquake, and she kept her two-year-old daughter alive by slicing her hand on broken glass and letting her daughter drink the blood. Then he went on to tell about Jesus' passion, filling in details that the biblical accounts leave blank.

132

Finally, he said, "If you want to be saved tonight, we love you, heaven is having a party, come forward and pray with a counselor. If you want to recommit your life tonight, we love you, heaven is having a party, come forward and pray with a counselor. The rest of you can go to the dining hall for juice and popcorn."

This kind of emotionally manipulative "evangelism" is an insult to the gospel — and to its recipients.

The ironic thing is that neither the overly cognitive nor the overly emotional approach to evangelism is particularly effective at making disciples. Both can be a lot like the seed planted in one of the bad soils of Jesus' parable in Luke 8: they blossom quickly but never take root, so they burn up and get choked out by weeds or eaten by the birds.

Postmodern students are attracted to ministries that don't rely too heavily on either the emotional or the cognitive but instead cut a middle path and exemplify the holistic, well-rounded nature of the gospel message.

More than ever we have to "walk our talk" and live out the imperatives of the gospel. What we look like as Christians matters as much as what we say in a postmodern context. When programming out ministries, for instance, we need to give as much time to developing experiences in which kids can work out their faith in real-life situations as we used to give to preparing our talks.

Right Here, Right Now

Another modern tendency we've fallen into in student ministry and evangelism is our desire to "close the deal." With our churches' modern approach, results are measured in numbers, and numbers come from our ability to get kids to fall in love with Jesus *fast*. Have you ever been called a "salesperson for Jesus" by someone in your congregation? Has your church ever been compared to a corporation? The fact is, modern American corporate culture has seeped inside the walls of the church, and it has affected our methodology.

In a corporation, growth is the highest value — and the quicker the better. While a client is being wined and dined by the vice president of sales, both parties *know* that the reason it's all taking place is so that the client will eventually sign the contract and order 100,000 widgets from the corporation. There is a mutual understanding — it's a game.

Our outreach nights, lock-ins, camps, and retreats have been much the same: we're going to wow the unchurched kids with big-time games, high-energy activities, and talented speakers. And then, at the end of the night, we're going to close the deal with a decision.

The problem is that it's not a mutual pact — the unchurched students don't know the goal of the whole event is *their conversion*.

Maybe we should have a disclaimer at the beginning of the event: "Please be aware, at the end of the night, we will be presenting you with a choice to follow Jesus – this evening may seem like all fun and games, but we do have a purpose here. We follow Christ, and we will be inviting you to join us." Lacking this preface, we're like the person who invites you over to their house for a "really great business opportunity," and only after three hours you discover that they want you for a pyramid scheme.

Faith in Christ is a *journey, a long-term thing*. Discipleship is a path that takes a lifetime to walk. A friend of mine once pondered, "I know the day I invited Jesus into my heart, but it was not until years later that I really decided to follow him – to make him Lord of my life. I wonder, when I get to heaven, when he will say that I was really saved…"

One obvious answer is that he was saved on a Friday about 2,000 years ago.

This answer is less facile than it may look. We may have to give up the whole notion of a "salvation date" or a "spiritual birthday" in this postmodern world. We must view evangelism not as a moment in time when individuals give their lives totally over to Christ, but as an invitation into a community of journeyers who are daily letting Christ take them in new directions of faithfulness. We must end the false dichotomy between justification and sanctification.

133

Since so much in a postmodern life is journey and experience, it seems only natural that faith should be as well. And when we look at the long and arduous journey of the original disciples, their battles with confusion, doubt, and denial, *journey* seems like a more appropriate metaphor for faith than signing a sales agreement, anyway.

We need to reclaim a reformed understanding of salvation. Ephesians says we were saved before foundation of the world. Sure, the concept of election is controversial, but I believe it's a miracle of God. I mean, dead people rising and blind people seeing? No youth ministry event can make that happen. That's a work of God. These days, the most offensive thing to me regarding the issue of witnessing and salvation is this idea that "anyone can come to faith in Christ if you share the gospel with them in the right way." Essentially that implies that if you don't close the deal, it's your fault! That's not the gospel. Our witnessing should spring forth from an overspill of joy and happiness and fellowship rather than a Pelagian, guilt-ridden duty. We proclaim good news — we don't "close deals."

Mark Driscoll

The Cult of Personality

One of the main criticisms of the modern, Baby Boomer, seeker-sensitive churches is they've been driven by the charismatic personalities of strong men. One might question whether the secret is being purpose-driven or seeker-sensitive, or if it's really putting an articulate, energetic man who is a great speaker and a good manager in charge of an affluent suburban church. Whatever the case, these are men who would probably succeed in almost any entrepreneurial endeavor — we're just fortunate that God gave them a passion for his church.

Unfortunately their charisma does not transfer to many of us. Hence, many a pastor has tried to implement these big church models only to find limited success or no success at all — at least as measured by the irredeemably modern yardstick of growth and numbers. Few of us have the combination of personality, work ethic, and managerial savvy that it takes to build a big church.

Or a big youth ministry. Many of us have tried these same models as they've been translated and marketed to student ministry — and, like our senior pastors, we've had a difficult time getting the formula to work in our churches.

Mark Yaconelli, who directs the Youth Ministry and Spirituality Project at San Francisco Theological Seminary, made an interesting observation recently. The reason many youth ministries go downhill after a "successful" youth worker leaves, he said, is not because that youth worker is the only one who could bring those students the gospel — it's because those kids gave their lives to the youth pastor rather than to Christ![30] Ouch!

In other words, there's a fine line between living out the incarnational witness of Jesus and leading students down a path in which the youth pastor's personal charisma is confused with Jesus' love.

Mark's comment alone should cause us to rethink our definition of "success." There are at least two different kinds of church planters. One kind wants to build big, "successful" churches and make a career out of it — and the churches rarely flourish when the planters leave.

134

The other type of planter wants to start a healthy church, empower the leadership — and then quietly move on. These planters even say this up front so no one has false expectations. This is a fairly new way to plant a church, and it is working. Chris Seay (formerly of Waco and now Houston, Texas) employs this approach, and the churches he planted are excellent examples of healthy, Christ-centered communities.

Of course, this seems to contradict what's written above: that youth workers should make long-term commitments to their churches (we should) — and that churches should make long-term commitments to their youth workers (they should). But we must guard against the cult of personality that can so easily happen between a 20- or 30-year-old youth worker and a group of students. Even if we're in it for the long haul, we must have the mind of the second church planter, building communities that will flourish long after we're gone.

In the communitarian environment prevalent in the postmodern world, we'll do well to rethink the personality-driven programs that many of us have used for years. Instead of scripted talks and didactic teachings every week, we must facilitate discussion and dialogue. Instead of making decisions and implementing them, we must be primarily about developing a team of leaders who see themselves as our colleagues instead of our employees. And we must constantly ask ourselves, "What will this ministry look like two years after I leave?"

135

In Ephesians 4:11-12a, Paul teaches, "It was he who gave some to be apostles, some to be prophets, some to be evangelists, and some to be pastors and teachers, *to prepare God's people for works of service.*" Note that Paul did not advocate that pastors and leaders do the work themselves. Yet empowering others for ministry is not a pastor's ultimate purpose. Before helping our students and staff calculate how God wants to work *through* them, our first goal should be to help them discover what God is doing *in* them.

Kara Powell

A Whole New Ballgame

As evangelists, Christians recently have believed that putting together a tight propositional argument was the primary means of converting an individual. While that may have worked in a modern world, we are transitioning into a new world where this propositional foundationalism will no longer hold sway.

In the middle of the 20th century, philosophers of many different stripes were coming to the same conclusion: "truth," as it was defined during the modern period, does *not* mean "that which bears the closest resemblance to reality." Since all of our conclusions are based on subjective interpretation of human observation, and since our already-held theories inevitably influence the observations we make, "truth" may be understood as that which best matches our experience of life and is most coherent, pragmatic, and intellectually justifiable.

136

HOLISM:

1. The theory that living matter or reality is made up of organic or unified wholes that are greater than the simple sum of their parts.

2. [Holism is] the doctrine that only whole language or whole theories or whole belief systems really have meanings, so that the meanings of smaller units — words sentences, hypotheses, predictions, discourses, dialogues, texts, thoughts, and the like — are merely derivative.

Therefore, while a solid, rational argument will always have some intellectual credibility in the process of evangelism, it is no longer checkmate. Now it only moves a knight.

In his effort to deconstruct foundationalism in the pursuit of knowledge, Harvard philosopher W.V.O. Quine proposed that a system of belief is not best understood as multiple layers of building blocks upon a foundation. Instead, he wrote –

> The totality of our so-called knowledge or beliefs, from the most casual matters of geography and history to the profoundest laws of atomic physics or even pure mathematics and logic, is a *man-made fabric* which impinges on experience only along the edges.[31]

137

In other words, anything we know, be it scientific thought or religious belief, is not formulated in a vacuum. All knowledge is arrived at holistically via our experiences.[32]

The wonderful thing about following Quine is that his new conception of acquiring knowledge by a combination of experience and reflection rather than air-tight logic frees us from the modern predilection to "prove" the faith. No longer must we feel compelled to show that the Bible is without error to an unbelieving student who, most probably, is going to look very suspiciously upon that kind of claim. Instead, we can invite this pre-Christian student to *experience* the truth of Scripture by inviting him into the life of our community.

And the fact is, *we* may feel that the evidence for God and Jesus demands a verdict, but postmodernism repudiates that: if *we* think the evidence demands a verdict, it's only because *we* are standing within the Christian tradition. To a student *outside* the Christian tradition, there may seem to be very little evidence, and it doesn't demand any kind of verdict.

The foundationalism of the modern period is running out of gas – it's time to reconceive Christian apologetics.

The Web of Belief

In attempting to build a new paradigm for 21st century evangelism and apologetics, we should note several characteristics of Quine's thought.

138

- The fabric, or "web of belief," is fashioned by human beings — there is no divinely inspired web. That is, any apologetic system that enables us to defend our Christianity in the face of an unbelieving world or an unbelieving student is a very human way to conceive of some aspect of knowledge (e.g., the providence of God) that is truly beyond our grasp. Probably the first thing we need to say to a postmodern student is that our tiny human brains can only comprehend a fraction of a scintilla of God's totality.

  The great thing about this characteristic is that it takes the pressure off us as evangelists-apologists. We youth workers don't have to go into a conversation with a non-Christian kid as though going into battle. And we do not have to develop air-tight arguments, like the perfect suit of armor. Instead, we're proposing an *ancient yet new way of life.*

- Instead of being based upon one indubitable truth-doctrine, the web has truths-doctrine distributed throughout. Therefore, if one truth-doctrine gets adjusted or overthrown by a new discovery, the web repairs itself by adjusting or tweaking other doctrines — "Reevaluation of some statements entails reevaluation of others, because of their logical interconnections."[33]

  In other words, the closer to the center of the web or fabric, the more theoretical the truth. Nancey Murphy has suggested that we call these central doctrines in the web its "hard core beliefs." Depending on the Christian community from which you hail, these might be the authority of Scripture, the divinity and humanity of Christ, and/or the triune nature of God. The closer to the edge of the web, the more tangible the doctrine — for example, that God is revealed in nature, that human life is sacred, and that God desires us to come into his presence through worship.

- The periphery of the web is human experience. This is where the ideas and doctrines of the Christian web connect with our day-to-day life experiences. In other words, our web is not only bound by our experiences with God, others, and creation, our system of belief is informed on all sides by what we see, hear, feel, and otherwise experience in the world.

  But a one-to-one correlation doesn't exist between an experience and a doctrine since each doctrine near the edge may be connected to experience at three or four points – "No particular experiences are linked with any particular statements in the interior of the field except indirectly through considerations of equilibrium affecting the field as a whole."[34] That means that each belief is tied to many real-life experiences.

139

- Reasoning is a two-way street instead of a one-way. In foundationalism, reasoning is always moving from the foundation up since the foundation is the indubitable, unquestionable basis of the entire system. Postmodernism has shown, however, that experience affects doctrine and doctrine affects experience, and the web scheme reflects this.

The Web of Belief

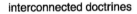
interconnected doctrines

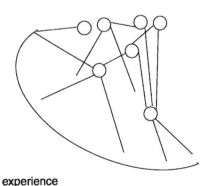

experience

140

Putting It to Use

This new epistemological scheme is neither divinely inspired nor is it the final word in apologetics — *it is simply a new way to think of the Christian system of belief.* It is a way to get our minds to move away from modern foundationalism toward a conception of faith that matches the way many in the world now think.

We now have a holistic way to measure and defend Christianity. Instead of matching our foundation with the foundations of other belief systems (e.g., the Bible is better than the *Qu'ran* and *Dianetics* and *The Celestine Prophecy*), we can match up our web with the webs of other religious systems on several criteria.

For instance, say you have entered into a dialogue with a student who has become enamored of Buddhism — she has read a lot about Buddhist beliefs and practices, and she has begun to practice Buddhist spirituality, both privately and with others. The first step in postmodern evangelism is to build a level of trust that she feels comfortable with — she needs to know that you will continue to care about her as a person even if she *never* accepts the tenets of Christianity.

One of the crucial issues for ministry today is the necessity of teaching a "new language." In many ways, becoming a Christian is much like learning a new language. Youth ministers would be well served by learning from ESL (English as a Second Language) instructors about the best ways to proceed.

Doug Pagitt

Secondly, the two of you have to agree to conceive of Christianity and Buddhism as two distinct webs – that, although the web is simply a metaphor, it is an apt metaphor that is helpful when speaking of belief systems. From that point on, your conversations might, over time, move along the following line of questions:

141

- *Which web is most coherent?* That is, which belief system has a thicker web of well-developed doctrines? Compare the teachings of the greatest Christian theologians with the greatest Buddhist theologians.

- *Which web displays more equilibrium?* That is, which system has more interconnections between doctrines? In the theological schemes, does either Buddhism or Christianity have weaknesses in the weight on one or two beliefs? Which one is more balanced?

- *Which web matches itself best with human experience?* Which fabric has the most connections between the interior belief structures and the periphery? When thinking of day-to-day life, does Christianity have more to offer, or does Buddhism?

- *Which web better repairs itself when breached?* Quine refers to this as repairing the planks of a boat while staying afloat in it. Which religion has a better track record with paradigm shifts? And which would respond better to a future, hypothetical shift?

The Final Analysis

Evangelism (proclaiming the Good News) and apologetics (defending the faith) must always be done in culturally appropriate ways. And in a world in which absolute, foundational truth is being overthrown in fields like mathematics, physics, philosophy, and language theory, it seems ludicrous that Christians would insist that ours is the one indubitably sure thing in the world.

142

What ultimately makes Christianity the best option? Maybe I'm being too "old-school modern," but I believe it's because Christianity is the most true. Jesus didn't merely call himself "the best option" – he declared himself "the truth" (John 14:6). It is our understanding of him as the truth that's imperfect. Just as humility requires us to admit our imperfect understanding of divine truth, honesty forces us to recognize that elements of truth exist in other religions.

Kara Powell

Better that we begin to speak of our Christian tradition, our theology, and our faith as the best option among many — the most adequate for human life and existence, the most intellectually coherent, the most true to real life experience, the most resilient. In the postmodern world, the Christian web of belief is one among many, so it does us little good to claim that it's the only option; people believe that they have a myriad of options. And neither should we claim to prove our system *conclusively*, because *everything* is now open to questions.

143

You may find this maddening — your inner voice may be screaming, "But Christ is the *only way!*" Indeed, from *within* the Christian faith he most clearly is. But to argue final, indubitable, absolute Truth in a world that doesn't believe that such a thing exists is like spitting into the wind: it is ineffective, and you look silly doing it.

The truth is, you can be a Christian without being a foundationalist — and you can share the gospel without using foundationalist arguments. We are not letting go of Christ, nor are we starting down the slippery slope that leads to liberalism. Instead, we are moving beyond the foundationalism that gave birth to liberalism and fundamentalism. We're living in a world that is giving up on foundations, so it is imperative that we find ways to talk about the gospel without relying upon foundations.

Let's enter into the cultural and academic conversations at the highest levels, ready to engage. Let us begin to churn out high school graduates who walk into Philosophy 101 freshman year in college and are ready — though they may not even know it — to defend Christianity in the postmodern dialogue.

5

A child of the Enlightenment, the seeker-sensitive movement in the evangelical church has allowed culture to define the methods by which the gospel is communicated. The same thing happened in mainline circles with religious experience. While both of these movements were appropriate for the modern context, postmodern youth ministers must take seriously the inherited speech, movements, and liturgies that make the Christian faith so rich.

the missing piece

146

Manderson, South Dakota, is at the heart of the Pine Ridge Reservation, in many ways the quintessential American Indian Reservation – it is home to the Oglala Lakota (Sioux) and the basis for dozens of books (*Bury My Heart at Wounded Knee* and *In the Spirit of Crazy Horse*) and movies (*Dances with Wolves* and *Thunderheart*). The Oglala Lakota are wonderfully generous and beautiful, albeit defeated, people.

In the 1970s and '80s, the people of Pine Ridge – and Indians across North America – began to realize that they were about to lose one of the elements essential to their otherness: *their language*. They realized that if they lost the Lakota language, they would be losing aspects of their culture and identity that would be irretrievable, and they would blend into mainstream American culture even more than they already had.

So they immediately began encouraging their elders to speak more Lakota in public; they taught Lakota in elementary and secondary schools; they made the language a part of the curriculum at their community college; DJs on the reservation's radio station, KILI, speak Lakota, and you now hear the language frequently in stores, government offices and restaurants, at meetings and gas stations. And subsequently there has been a rebirth of Lakota culture on the reservation and around the world.

English is still the primary language of the Lakota people. And the Lakota children want to speak English, because that's the language of the outside world, of TV, radio, business, and culture. But now, as the children grow older, they'll come to appreciate the importance of *their* language.

In Pinky's Store in Manderson, it's easy to make friends with many of the people who pass through. And nothing brings a smile to their faces like asking, "How do you say *popsicle* in Lakota?" Or slipping a Lakota word into a conversation. They really love it if you name your dog Shunka, which is Lakota for *dog*.

It brings them joy when someone outside their community uses their language, because it validates their cultural identity; it validates their identity because their language sets them apart. Their language sets them apart because it is uniquely *theirs* – it's part of what makes them Lakota.

Similarly, the Christian language – words, concepts, traditions, doctrines, values – is what sets us apart. And in an effort to avoid another generation of Christians who are too accommodating of culture and somewhat uninformed about what makes Christians unique, we must teach and embody this Christian language.

I disagree. The destructive force among the Boomer ministries of the '80s wasn't primarily a language problem. It went much deeper than that. It was the construction of a religion of self-reliance — one that had absolutely no need for the person and continuing work of Jesus Christ. It's not our language that ultimately sets us apart as Christians, but the living, embodied, risen Lord Jesus. All the other religions of the world rely on the externals of language — doctrines, concepts, and traditions — to set them apart. If we are going to have something truly different to offer, it will have to be the Christ who lived, died, rose from the dead, and reigns in our hearts — not statements about Christ or even values based on what Christ said.

147

While it's definitely helpful to teach nonbelievers Christian vocabulary, principles, and especially the history behind Christian practices, let's not fool ourselves into believing that *information* is equivalent to *transformation*. That's a mistake the modern church has made for more than 300 years.

The Scriptures are clear (John 1 and 1 John): the Word is first and foremost a *person*, not words, concepts, traditions, doctrines, or even values. In Philippians 2:4-11, it's not a manuscript or vocabulary book that God sends to transform the world. It's not words or concepts or religious ideas. It is God's very own son.

Sally Morgenthaler

Making Disciples

Our primary task as youth workers is to make disciples. And making disciples is something that we have worked hard at over the last few decades. Great strides have been made in teaching students how to pray, how to read their Bibles, and how to pursue God — for the first time in the 2,000-year history of the Christian Church, there is a group of pastors who have dedicated their lives exclusively to the spiritual formation of youth.

148

As much as curricula and methods and recipes abound for youth evangelism, there are probably double that for youth discipleship. Why? Perhaps because discipling youth is such a daunting and confusing task. Or maybe it's because we don't really know what a disciple looks like. Most likely, it's a combination of the two.

The question we must ask is, "Are we developing well-rounded disciples?" That is, have we emphasized the conversion and holy living of our students at the expense of teaching the Christian language?

Reasserting the importance, perhaps even priority, of *doing* discipleship. After all, the disciples recovers the biblical call to did not learn that Jesus was the Messiah and then decide to follow him. Rather, they realized his messiahship by following him.

Jonathan R. Wilson, "Toward a New Evangelical Paradigm of Biblical Authority" in Timothy R. Philips and Dennis L. Okham, eds., *The Nature of Confession*, 157

In the 14th chapter of Luke, Jesus makes clear some of the requirements of a disciple: leaving family behind, giving up worldly possessions, and carrying the cross. But what sustenance do our students need in order to make these difficult commitments? As we continue to seek an answer to this question, let's begin by looking at the word itself.

The word *disciple* has a long history, through Latin, French, and Old English. Its roots mean "to learn" and probably "to drive toward a goal." With this in mind, our task — with God's help — is to turn out *learners, followers,* even *scholars* of the Christian faith.[35]

149

There was a time when every educated person, no matter how professedly unbelieving or secular, knew the actual text from Genesis to Revelation with a thoroughness that would put contemporary ministers and even theologians to shame.

George A. Lindbeck, "The Church's Mission to a Postmodern Culture" in Frederic B. Burnham, ed., *Postmodern Theology: Christian Faith in a Pluralist World,* 38

The goal of youth ministry ought to be bringing about the Kingdom of God on earth as it is in heaven. Youth ministers need to be extremely careful not to replace the concept of being a Christian — based on the global, historical church — with an oversimplified understanding of being a disciple in an American context.

Doug Pagitt

Three caveats: first, *language* in this chapter refers to much more than words. While the actual verbiage of the faith will be considered, *language* also includes liturgy, rites, theology, ethics – the whole web of belief. In other words, *language* refers to *the whole of Christian life*. Just as nonverbal cues constitute three-quarters of the way human beings communicate, so the words of Christian faith are only a part of our entire language system.

150

Second, the word *doctrine* may carry a great deal of baggage for you. Many Christian youth workers will say, "All that matters is that you love and follow Jesus." But that statement itself is doctrine, and it's a good doctrine! While this sentiment should always be primary in our ministries, we must broaden our discussion if we are to teach and defend our faith in the postmodern era. Doctrine, in fact, is the way we use words to communicate the whole Christian life. So let's try to take a fresh look at doctrine.

Correct doctrine is *not* the way through the narrow gate that Jesus describes in the Sermon on the Mount. He makes it clear, as does the entire witness of Scripture, that obedience is the way down that hard road. But as we journey together down this faith road, doctrine and theology encompass the ways we talk to each other about what we are experiencing – Christians have been talking to one another for 2,000 years. Doctrine is the language of the journey. As we will see in the next chapter, novel ways to teach doctrine exist, but first we must see why the teaching of doctrine is imperative to making disciples.

Third, we must immediately distance ourselves from the "God talk," slogans, and insider jargon sometimes called Christianese. This kind of language neither reflects the depth of Christian theology and faith nor does it bolster the faith of people within or without the church. Usually it's just lazy and irresponsible speech, and it usually only serves to make non-Christians – or just those outside your denomination – feel excluded.

For instance, a group of three youth workers who have seen a type of revival happen in their town recently came to our youth pastors' networking lunch. In the course of their presentation, they kept referring to students who were *saved* and others who were *unsaved* – we finally stopped them and asked, "What exactly do you mean by *saved*?" Their definitions of these words – as well as for *revival* and *believer* – were narrow and evangelically slanted. What's more, they assumed everyone in the room shared their definitions. But the Catholic and Methodist youth workers did not. In the same way, mainline protestants fall into the same trap by calling their churches "open and affirming" or "social justice congregations." Within their small circles, these phrases may have meaning, but in the broader, ecumenical circle of orthodox Christianity, these phrases serve only to establish a group of insiders and make everyone else feel like outsiders.

The doctrinal terminology that has been the meat on the plate of Christian theology for 2,000 years must be used, and indeed celebrated, in our youth ministries. But the insider lingo of our particular branch of Christianity is more like parsley – it may add some color to the plate, but it has no nutritional value.

In summary, while much of the emphasis on discipleship has been well-placed, youth ministry has lacked focus in the area of doctrinal content. And, as we shall see, *post-modernism has shown that the content of a belief system is inseparable from and dependent upon its language.* That is, a word makes no sense unless it is part of a sentence, and a sentence makes no sense unless it is part of a language.

Not-So-Crazy Ludwig[36]

The preeminent philosopher of language of the last 150 years was Ludwig Wittgenstein (1889-1951). After he died, several of his works were published, including *The Blue and Brown Books* (1958), a compendium of class notes taken by his students at Cambridge from 1933 to 1935.

Here Wittgenstein poses a fairly tricky idea: a *"sentence has sense only as a member of a system of language; as one expression within a calculus."* [37] In other words, a sentence cannot stand alone – if it does it's meaningless. Any statement, sentence, or proposition – such as, "For God so loved the world that he gave his only son, that whoever believes in him shall not perish but have eternal life" – derives its meaning from its place within the whole scheme of the language.

When you first heard that sentence, you already held communally agreed-upon definitions of *God*, *love*, *believes*, and *life*. Without these definitions, John 3:16 would either be meaningless to you or have an entirely different meaning.

A belief statement is meaningless without the context of a language.

Wittgenstein's classic, *Philosophical Investigations,* was written in the last years of his life and published in 1963. Here Wittgenstein goes one step further than anyone had before, establishing what has become one of the hallmarks of postmodern thought. *Language,* he argues, *is only useful in community – that is, all speech acts are really parts of language games,* the rules of which are mutually agreed upon by the community in which the individual is speaking.

151

From Wittgenstein to Lindbeck

This is a radical departure from modern language theory. No longer is the individual expressing her own thought about what she has sensed in the world. Instead, she is playing a game with words in a way she knows (because she has been indoctrinated into the language game by her culture) that others in her community will understand.

152

A decade later, J. L. Austin furthered this philosophical revolution at Oxford when he developed the idea that "language ordinarily relates to the world, to the deeds and attitudes and standpoints of the speaker and hearer, and to the employed linguistic conventions of the community."[38] That is, language is communal.

It may seem that, with this discussion of language, we've ventured a long way from youth ministry, but this revolution in the philosophy of language has enormous implications for the way we minister to youth. We start to turn in that direction by looking to George Lindbeck, a theologian at Yale University, who wrote the groundbreaking *The Nature of Doctrine* in 1984.[39] In it he applies Wittgenstein's categories to religious language.

After noting the shortcomings of the experiential-expressivist model, Lindbeck proposes the cultural-linguistic model of language. A religion, he writes, functions differently with regard to its language than anything else: "Its doctrines, cosmic stories, or myths, and ethical directives are integrally related to the rituals it practices, the sentiments or experiences it evokes, the actions it recommends, and the institutional form it develops."[40]

This is a pretty big piece of meat to chew on, so let's cut it into smaller pieces.

First, let's look at what Lindbeck says religious discourse *is not:* a response to the human experience of God in the world. For instance, when we pray, we're not just emoting whatever comes to our minds about God and his relationship with us. Neither, when someone writes a book on prayer, is he categorizing what is *true* about prayer. Instead, Lindbeck states, all religious speech is like any other language: *it is utilizing the words and symbols that have been agreed upon by the community in ways that have been agreed upon by the community.*

It's like, "Which came first, the chicken or the egg?" Modern thinkers said the experience comes first and the language of faith is an attempt to express that experience. The postmodern counters that the language is first and our religious experiences are categorized by the words and phrases of our faith community.

The Accommodationist Turn

Thus, in Lindbeck's view, the 20th-century church made a mistake when it set about translating the language of Christianity into a more palatable and understandable language for the average Joe and Jane. The mainline Protestant church took this turn in the mid-20th century, following the lead of H. Richard Niebuhr, who detailed several ways that Christians and the church can interact with culture, and many of his mainline peers took the road of cultural accommodation in order to hold their places in the public square. The problem is this accommodationist model in many instances led to the watering down of the gospel, not unlike the Lakota experiencing the weakening of their culture.

153

Ironically, the evangelical church took a similar turn in the 1980s and '90s, led by some seeker-sensitive megachurches. In this model, words like *sin* and *justification* were avoided in worship and entry-level classes on the assumption that those terms will be a turnoff to Joe and Jane who are not versed in Christianese. Worship was even bifurcated in some churches, with a seeker-friendly service on Sunday morning and believer worship midweek.

We just need to be mindful that, while translation is necessary, it's also very dangerous--
because in leaning over to speak to the modern world, a lot of times we fall face-down
into it. We end up not saying anything the world couldn't hear by reading Dear Abby. In
classes like Intro to Psychology, the students complain that the whole first semester is
spent doing nothing but learning new vocabulary, and I say to them, "Well good, maybe

154

you won't complain when you come to church!
When I say redemption, it isn't fair for you to
say, 'Wait a second. I'm a 20th-century person
from Illinois. You can't use a word like Trinity
with me.'" I, as a preacher, need to say, "Be
quiet. Write this word down. I'll teach you how
to spell it and how to use it correctly." That's a

big deal.

William Willimon, "Preaching & Theology in the New Millennium" in *Cutting Edge* (Volume 4, Number 1, Winter 2000), 4

At least one prominent Christian author has referred to this trend as dumbing down worship.[41] The reasoning behind this turn in the modern church was that heavy Christian theology and terminology would be unattractive to the seeker not versed in such talk or who had a negative church experience earlier in life. So avoiding Christian language was a way to protect against unnecessarily turning Joe and Jane away.

Many youth ministries followed suit, tailoring their programs to two different constituencies: the Christian student and the non-Christian student. And the outreach events to the non-Christian students were only peripherally related to the church – Christian students were told to bring their nonbelieving friends to these events. Then discipleship began *after* the nonbeliever became a believer.

This linear model (evangelize ▶ convert ▶ disciple) is a reflection of the modern predilection toward linear simplicity. But in a postmodern world, the process of making disciples must be seen as more holistic, or at least as less quantifiable and more organic. (Postmodernism suggests that even the separation of this chapter and the last seems like an artificial distinction between evangelism and discipleship!)

Lindbeck's Conclusions

As a remedy for the cultural accommodation of mainline and evangelical churches, Lindbeck proposes conclusions that are revolutionary for Christian discipleship and youth ministry:

> How, as modern Christians often put it, does one preach the gospel in a dechristianized world?…The [postmodern] method of dealing with this problem is bound to be unpopular among those chiefly concerned to maintain or increase the membership and influence of the church. *This method resembles ancient catechesis more than modern translation. Instead of redescribing the faith in new concepts, it seeks to teach the language and practices of the religion to potential adherents.* This has been the primary way of transmitting the faith and winning converts…down through the centuries…Only after [catechumens] had acquired proficiency in the alien Christian language and form of life were they deemed able intelligently and responsibly to profess faith, to be baptized.[42]

155

In other words, *we need to teach students the language of Christianity.* As followers of Jesus, we have a unique and distinct way of viewing the world and of talking about our faith experience. And, over a history of several thousand years, we have developed a language to be able to speak, represent, and reflect upon ourselves, God, the cosmos, and our experience of the three.

156

Tony states that we need to teach students the language of Christianity. I agree. But I believe we need to take this a step further. Before we teach the language, we need to deconstruct much of the Christian terminology that postmodern teenagers know — then reconstruct these terms biblically. To a postmodern teenager, *Armageddon* is a Bruce Willis movie, not a geographic location in Israel. An angel can fall in love with humans — and even become human — as in *City of Angels*. Satan can look like Al Pacino (*The Devil's Advocate*) or Elizabeth Hurley (*Bedazzled*). They know terms like *anti-Christ* and end-times theology from movies like *End of Days* and from Marilyn Manson songs. Theological language is being taught every day, yet it's usually a far cry from biblical truth. This means an extra step for us, as we deconstruct language first.

Dan Kimball

Some might argue that *all* talk of God is translation because God is so far out of our ability to perceive him. True. All talk of God falls short of capturing his infinite and eternal being. But this is not to say that we should never talk *of* him. Though Gnostics claim that talk of God is impossible because he is the Unknowable, this is an argument that won't get very far with youth workers — for we have committed our lives to the communication of the Good News.

Biblical literacy, though not sufficient, is indispensable. This literacy does not consist of historical, critical knowledge about the Bible. Nor does it consist of theological accounts, couched in nonbiblical language, of the Bible's teachings and meanings. Rather it is the patterns and details of its sagas and stories, its images and symbols, its syntax and grammar, which need to be internalized if one is to imagine and think scripturally. And when one proceeds to imagine and think scripturally, one may in fact use very little actual biblical terminology. What is to be promoted are those approaches which increase familiarity with the actual text.

George A. Lindbeck, "The Church's Mission to a Postmodern Culture" in Frederic B. Burnham, ed., *Postmodern Theology: Christian Faith in a Pluralist World*, 51-52

157

Others may say that Lindbeck's thesis unrealistically pushes us all to learn Greek and Hebrew so that we can converse about scriptural matters with the actual words and language in which Scripture was written. Only then would we be able to talk of God without translation.

Remember, this is not what Lindbeck, Wittgenstein, and others mean by *language*. They mean a system of communication that includes all Christian theology, thought, words, rituals, rites, worship, songs, et cetera. That is, the way language and ideas work together to form a unified whole (or web or fabric). All Christian belief, then, is a unified whole, and Lindbeck's point is the individual points in the web *matter* – it *matters* how you say what you say about the Christian faith.

Just As If...

For instance, the doctrine of justification is a weighty and somewhat difficult theological concept, especially for a high school student. Louis Berkhof, a preeminent Reformed theologian, defines justification thus: *"Justification is a judicial act of God, in which he declares, on the basis of the righteousness of Jesus Christ, that all the claims of the law are satisfied with respect to the sinner."*[43]

158

Far be it for me to quarrel with Berkhof, but reading Tony's discussion here, the thought strikes me: defining justification à la Berkhof might not be the most helpful way of understanding it — or helping students understand it. Instead we might be better off seeing justification as a part of an extended biblical metaphor that uses the language of courts and judges (human inventions, elements of most human cultures) to tell us something true and important about God and the gospel. In other words, God was good and just and holy way before humans invented judges and courts and lawyers (!) and judgments...including justification. But since we've created these things, they can serve as useful images (properly understood) to help us understand God. So rather than merely defining a term such as justification using abstractions, how about creating a concrete story or scenario about a judge (as Jesus would have done in his parables) that helps students think about a judge's desires, goals, values, commitments, and duties? From the context of that story, we could help teens understand and feel more poignantly the import of justification.

Brian McLaren

As youth workers, we might think, "Not only is *justification* difficult for *me* to understand, it may be beyond some high school students' intellectual capabilities. And surely it is boring, irrelevant, and off-putting. If I try to teach about *justification*, they'll be so turned off that they'll never come back."

So, one common response has often been to translate justification into a pithy phrase that students can grab onto: *just-as-if* I'd never sinned. Of course, when we compare this to Berkhof's definition, we can see how this slogan falls short of summing up the true depth of justification.

159

Another example is *sin*. Although at the top of the list of essential church doctrines, *sin* has been changed to *missing the mark*, *falling short*, and even *making a mistake* in the interest of being seeker-sensitive. While each of these phrases captures an aspect of our human depravity and penchant for transgression, none captures the full essence of *sin*.

The problem isn't with using these phrases to help our kids understand sin — indeed, they can be helpful teaching tools. The problem is when our students are taught in such a way that they *replace sin* with a catchphrase like "missing the mark" — or *justification* with "just as if I'd never sinned."

We do our students a disservice if we lead them to believe that Christianity and its essential doctrines are simple and easy to comprehend. Life is messy, and faith is a tricky, complex thing. That's one of the paradoxes inherent to Christianity: on one hand, Jesus told us to come to him as little children; on the other hand, it's no easy matter — intellectually or spiritually — to follow a crucified savior.

160

I couldn't agree more — but just hold on. Youth ministry has always been wedded to some kind of popularized-relevant-entertaining method of sharing faith. Can we make this kind of adjustment without unraveling our whole network of festivals, publishing companies, ministries, and businesses? I suppose we could just switch track and develop ambiguous, hard-to-understand ideas, games, and resources. But isn't that what many churches have been doing for years and calling it *worship*?

Pete Ward

I don't think we should always assume that the contemporary church at its scholarly best has all that great an understanding of words or concepts such as *sin*. For example, *sin* is commonly understood in our churches in a fundamentally medieval sense, where it's primarily an offense against a dignitary. Or it might be linked in many church contexts with an almost Platonic concept of the fall, where being physical and human and creaturely gets mixed up with being sinful.

So just as our pop definitions of these profound realities can be skewed (e.g., sin is missing the mark), so our more traditional understandings can represent the full, biblical picture in imbalanced or distorted ways. This is why we must always remain in the mode of being disciples — learners, students, apprentices, always open to correction and new understanding — rather than experts or know-it-alls.

Brian McLaren

In a postmodern world, we must exhibit authenticity and integrity as we teach students the essential tenets of the faith. If we oversimplify things, they will be blown away when they go into college or the working world and find that life and faith are not as simple as we led them to believe. Better that they're confronted with the rigorous complexities of faith *now* — in a community of faith where they can ask questions and work through spiritual dilemmas.

161

I fully agree. We recently went through a series at Graceland on Romans 6 through 8, spending a whole night just on terms like *justification* and *condemnation* and their meanings. I felt like I was teaching an English class, and the notes we handed out looked like a page from a dictionary! But much to my surprise, the response was overwhelmingly positive — in fact we had to make extra copies for several weeks afterward to meet the demand for information. Indeed there is a hunger and thirst among young people to understand the language of our faith.

Dan Kimball

My observations of students nationwide tells me that only 25 to 50 percent of the average high school ministry's graduates will integrate themselves in a college church or parachurch ministry. The rest leave the church, maybe never to return. If you're alarmed by these statistics and their implications for your teen disciples, pay attention to Tony's warning. Expose your students now to the spiritual and ethical quagmire they'll encounter in college. They should be just as challenged to think in your high school ministry as they will be in their freshman philosophy course.

Kara Powell

Big C and small c

162

At our church, we celebrate the Lord's Supper on the first Sunday of every month. And whenever we celebrate communion or baptism, we confess our faith together, usually with the Apostles' Creed. Not long ago, I was teaching our ninth graders about the meaning of the Creed, and, as usual, they were hung up on the line "I believe in…the holy, catholic church."

Tony misses the point here. The word *Catholic* is of no more value in our local language pattern than *global* or *universal*.

Doug Pagitt

The word *catholic* – with a small *c* – I told them, means *universal*. Although it's related to the big C version in *Roman Catholic*, it's akin to the difference between *Yankees* and *yankees*: one stands for a baseball team and the other stands for everyone north of the Mason-Dixon line.

Well, I happened to miss staff meeting the next Wednesday morning, and the pastoral staff talked about two former Roman Catholics who had approached them and objected to the use of the word *catholic* in the Creed. To avoid any hurt feelings, the staff decided to follow the practice of some churches and change the Creed to, "I believe in…the holy Christian church."

So the Creed was altered without my knowledge, and it was recited as such on the first Sunday of the next month. And our ninth graders were beside themselves!

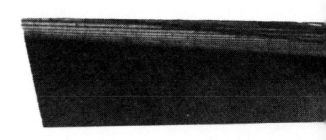

I invited our senior pastor to come to the group, and the students asked him, "Don't you know what *catholic* really means? It means *universal!*" David explained to them the dilemma of the former Roman Catholics in the congregation, and the ninth graders replied, *"Then you should teach them what "catholic" with a small c means!"*

This is a prime example of the postmodern penchant for connection with tradition. These postmodern ninth graders inherently realized that the traditions and history of our faith hold life that is lost when translated into hypercontemporary language. They realize that you cannot change the Apostles' Creed willy-nilly. They realize that *catholic* is one of *our* words, and we dare not lose it.

Conversely, after some study and reflection on the Lord's Prayer, our pastoral staff decided to changed "debts and debtors" (a.k.a., "trespasses and those who have trespassed against us") to "forgive us our *sins* as we forgive those *who sin against us."* We decided that *debts* and *trespasses* are not *our* words – they are not necessarily words of the church that should be saved in the Lord's Prayer. In fact, we decided that they have taken on so much superfluous cultural meaning that they actually hinder people from understanding the message of the prayer. Finally, we determined that *sin* is the closest word we have for the concept of *opheilemata* in Matthew 6:12.

It may seem highly subjective and fickle to hang on to *catholic* and teach students its true meaning but let go of *debts* and *trespasses.* It is subjective – subjective to our context and culture and our students and our congregation. The word *thy* holds lots of meaning to someone who speaks Middle English but is almost void of meaning today. *Debts* has changed in meaning over the years. *Sin* is *our* word. The postmodern way will be for each of our communities of faith to determine what language is worth saving and teaching and what language is archaic and outdated.

163

Last Words

By the time they are bar- and bat-mitzvahed at age 13, Jewish boys and girls know most of the symbolism and language of Judaism. Because they're in the cultural minority, Jews take the catechism of their young very seriously — every young Jewish person who ignores the tenets of their faith brings the Jewish people one person closer to extinction. The same goes for the Lakota people. Here are examples of middle schoolers speaking Hebrew and Lakota, and we're often afraid that our students cannot handle *justification*!

Christians are sitting on the most rich, elaborate, and beautiful symbolic language in God's creation, but we seem afraid to teach it to our young people. Every element of the liturgy has meaning, whether you're in a Roman Catholic, Lutheran, Reformed, Anglican, or Free Church setting. Everything the priest wears symbolizes something; every gesture he makes during Mass has theological significance; every word spoken from a prayer book or a hymnal or the Bible has rich history. And postmodern students *want to* know these symbols — they *want* to touch the past.

164

As youth workers, one of our jobs is to teach students the truth of the historic Christian doctrines, not to replace them with *Reader's Digest* theology.

It is crucial that we continue to produce theologians, in fact, postmodern theologians. We ought to be leery of any innuendo that would characterize current theology as lightweight or "Reader's Digest."

Doug Pagitt

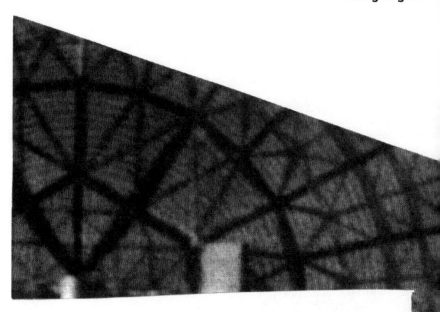

This is a very difficult proposition. For centuries, the creeds and catechisms were embedded in the bedrock of Western civilization – the idea of *justification* or *sin* was practically in our blood. But that bedrock has eroded – or at least broken off. Orthodox Christian doctrine is no longer taught or even embodied in society, school – or even in most families. It's no wonder that youth ministry has become a profession in the last 30 years – we're practically the only ones left who can teach and live out the deep, sacred truths of Jesus Christ. Therefore, we must take this task most seriously, not slipping into practices that dilute the profundity of our faith.

To do this, many of us are going to have to go back to school; we're going to have to learn for ourselves more about our rich Christian heritage, about the thoughts and ideas of theologians and pastors from around the world and from throughout the ages. But what could be more rewarding?

165

Lest we get too tied up in theory, this chapter offers some ideas regarding specific, postmodern-oriented discipleship programs as they work in a particular church setting. By participating in some rites of passage, students can learn the context of the faith even as they experience the love of God in a community environment. Recovery of a few other ancient practices is also discussed.

6

the how of discipleship

168

Once upon a time there was a 16-year-old named Lucius.[44] Lucius lived in Anagni, a small hill town south of Rome, in A.D. 296. The father of his friend, Marcus, frequently traveled to Rome on business and had become a Christian through his business contacts there.

Lucius had known of Christianity, but it wasn't until Marcus's father converted that he realized there was a good-sized band of followers of this new religion right in his own town. Marcus followed in his father's footsteps and became a Christian, too. Now as they daily tended the olive trees outside the city walls, Marcus told Lucius about his excitement at following Christ.

Ultimately convinced that "The Way" Marcus described was more desirable than the combination of household gods and imperial deities his family followed, Lucius agreed to let Marcus pray for him one day on the hillside. During that prayer, Lucius felt something he had never before experienced — it seemed that God himself was there!

Lucius said that he would like to join the Christian community of Anagni. Marcus was overjoyed, and he set up an appointment for Lucius to meet Gaius, one of the elders of the Anagni church.

Gaius and Lucius began a long and involved mentoring program. For *two years*, Gaius met with Lucius twice a week. One of the meetings concerned the theology and doctrines of the followers of Christ. Lucius was schooled in Jesus' teachings, his fulfillment of the Old Testament prophecies, the meaning of Easter, and the writings of the Apostles. The other weekly meeting focused on prayer – mainly Gaius praying for Lucius and exorcising him of demons. Occasionally all of those who were in the same boat as Lucius – the catechumens – gathered for teaching from the Bishop Antoninus, the head of the Anagni church.

169

CATECHISM:
A book giving a brief summary of the basic principles of Christianity in question-and-answer form.

CATECHUMEN:
One who is receiving rudimentary instruction in the doctrines of Christianity; a neophyte; in the primitive church, one officially recognized as a Christian, and admitted to instruction preliminary to admission to full membership in the church.

170

A big step came when Gaius invited Lucius to his first Sunday morning worship gathering. As Lucius walked in, he was overcome with anxiety – was he making the right choice? How would these people treat him? And why were they secretive about what they believed and where they met?

Most of his fears were quickly relieved. Lucius was greeted warmly by the hundred or so Christians who had gathered. It turned out that all of the Christians in Anagni had put their money together and purchased this house – for many years they had met in different members' homes, but three years ago they gathered enough to purchase a house to be used solely by the church.

At the beginning of the ceremony, Marcus stood up and introduced Lucius, his friend who desired to follow Christ. Emotion swirled in Lucius when he heard Marcus say this about him – and something inside told him he was making the best choice of his life.

The first part of the worship ceremony was kind of confusing, but Lucius liked it. Different people read from what they called the Law and the Prophets, they all sang songs and hymns together, and almost everyone took a turn at praying out loud. Bishop Antoninus then read from a letter. He spent about half an hour commenting on this letter, and he often referred to "the Apostles" as he spoke. What the bishop said made some sense to Lucius because of what he had learned over the last two years, and he already liked it a whole lot more than the annual ceremonies at the temple of Jupiter.

At the end of these comments, everyone started singing another hymn, but a few of the worshippers got up to leave. Gaius leaned over to Lucius and said to go with them, and he promised to explain more later. Lucius got up and left the main room, too, but he could hear what was taking place in the central room. The bishop said something about bread and wine…

Lucius' Journey

For many months this went on – Lucius was allowed to stay for the first half of worship and then had to withdraw to the peripheral room while "the baptized" participated in the Lord's Supper. And Lucius continued to meet with Gaius at least twice a week.

About six weeks before Easter of his third year of catechism, Gaius told Lucius that he was ready for the next step. At the worship celebration that Sunday, Lucius and a half dozen others were presented to the church no longer as catechumens but as "candidates for baptism." Gaius was asked by Bishop Antoninus if Lucius had been sincerely following Christ – if he had looked after the widows and orphans, visited the sick, and performed other good works. Gaius responded that yes, Lucius had lived a life exemplary of a follower of Christ.

Suddenly, the rigor of the program increased tenfold: Lucius was told to fast three times a week. He met with Gaius daily for exorcism, prayer, and teaching. And it seemed that Gaius was examining *every corner* of Lucius' life. In addition, he and the other catechumens were invited to participate in special liturgical rites including candle-lighting and foot-washing.

On the night before Easter, Lucius and the rest of the catechumens stayed up all night, fasting, hearing much of the story of Scripture, and keeping vigil. Late into the night (actually, early in the morning) Lucius heard all of the biblical stories of God's providence through water (creation, Noah, the Red Sea, Jonah, prophets, Jesus' baptism, and the baptisms recorded in Acts). And at sunrise, he stripped off all his clothes and joined the bishop and the other catechumens in front of the baptismal pool at the center of the house.

Bishop Antoninus asked Lucius, "Do you renounce Satan and all his ways?"

"I renounce them," Lucius replied.

Then the bishop anointed Lucius' head with the oil of exorcism, meaning that all demons and devils had been removed from Lucius. Lucius then followed Bishop Antoninus into the pool where he was asked, "Do you believe in the Father?"

172

"I believe." And he was immersed.

"Do you believe in the Son?"

"I believe." And he was immersed.

"Do you believe in the Spirit?"

"I believe." And he was immersed.

Lucius climbed out of the water and put his clothes back on. His emotions swirling, he followed the rest of the believers into the main room. There Bishop Antoninus laid hands on Lucius, praying that he would be open to the mystery of the sacraments, anointed him with the oil of thanksgiving and gave him the holy kiss of peace.

Then – *finally* – Lucius and the other newly baptized believers got to join the rest of the church at communion. After receiving the body and blood of the Lord for the first time, Lucius was offered the kiss of peace by everyone in the church. And finally, a taste of milk and honey was dropped on his tongue.

Three years and an incredible journey after that innocent prayer in the olive grove, Lucius was a member of Christ's holy church!

The Embattled Church

This account is what it might have been like to be matriculated into the Christian community of a small Roman town before A.D. 313 – before Constantine granted Christianity most-favored-religion status. It was no easy road! And notice that there is no dichotomy between evangelism and discipleship. Hippolytus, an early church historian, describes a thorough and difficult process before joining the Christian body. Reflecting on the process described above, Richard Osmer writes–

173

> The practice of initiation was designed to prepare prospective members for participation in a community that was *embattled*. It was a lengthy and demanding process. Ironically, this demanding process of initiation was offered precisely as the church was growing in leaps and bounds. This practice has much to teach the contemporary church about the importance of holding together catechetical instruction, spiritual direction, and liturgical formation.[45]

I believe there really is something important in all of this. But the reason why people were beating down the door to get into the church was because the culture of early Christianity was seen as being civilizing and superior to the bankruptcy of paganism and philosophy. Yet I'm not at all sure we can make the same claim for what goes on in our churches today. Are we self-evidently superior culturally? Are people turning to us because we offer solutions for social and political ills? I don't think so. In these circumstances what we offer may just turn out to be the equivalent to nailing our doors shut as we huddle together in the sanctuary.

Pete Ward

But after Constantine converted, the road to baptism changed dramatically. Instead of meeting in house churches that were meant to blend into the surrounding architecture, the Emperor had enormous and stately basilicas built to house hundreds of worshipers. The churches could hardly deal with the influx of converts, and so the catechumenal period was shortened, first to one year, and eventually to the six weeks of Lent.

174

Traditionalism is the dead faith of the living;

But that was *after* the Emperor had publicly confessed his faith in Christ. The question for us today is *do we have a Christian emperor or a pagan emperor*? Is our world more like pre-313 or post-313? Most commentators would say that we are living in a world more similar to the one before Christianity was the official religion of western culture — for the church is once again *embattled*. Our "emperor" may well be culture, for culture teaches us our norms (what is acceptable and what is not) more than any political leader. If that is so, the Christian community will continue to be marginalized and embattled.

175

tradition is the living faith of the dead.

Unknown

As youth workers, we must take the process of initiation into the Christian community far more seriously. First of all, most individuals who convert to Christianity do so before they turn 20, that is, *when they are in our ministries.* And secondly, as we have said before, *if we don't teach them, no one will.*

176

Tony emphasizes how to teach discipleship. Alongside this must come modeling a disciple's life. This task is crucial in urban areas when it comes to racism. Many young blacks and Latinos are daily the targets of racial prejudice. In following Christ more closely, issues of race are ever-present. They ask hard, painful questions. But mostly they watch to see how the leaders deal with racism.

Derek Perkins is black, and I'm Latino. Together we run an urban youth ministry. We asked one of our students — an African American young man who's recognized in our community as a racial peacemaker — how he learned to be a reconciler. I expected him to talk about Bible studies, prayer times, and history lessons. But this is what he said:

"I saw people like you and Derek not just trying to help your own people, but treating both blacks and Latinos the same. I remember the meetings with you and Derek where neither of you took sides on the issues of race. When we youths were clearly divided along racial lines, the way y'all fixed it made sense."

His response stopped me cold — all that time he had paid attention to what we *did* and *said*, not what we taught. From him I learned that, yes, we teach discipleship, but the greatest impact on young people may be what they catch on their own.

Rudy Carrasco

The Curious Case of Confirmation

Confirmation. The very word provokes a litany of reactions: boring, irrelevant, outdated. Indeed, recent surveys by the Episcopalian and Presbyterian (P.C.U.S.A.) churches have shown that only 43 to 50 percent of their Confirmands are still going to church (six times a year) by the time they're 40 years old.[46]

But the problem may be with *how* confirmation has been done over the last half century rather than with confirmation itself. In fact, breathing new life into this ancient rite may be exactly the way to teach our students the vocabulary of the Christian faith.

Confirmation was developed as a program (and a sacrament in the Roman Catholic and Anglican traditions) as baptism and catechism were separated. Infant baptism became more commonly practiced between the fifth and eighth centuries, yet the church continued to recognize the importance of catechism, or discipleship training, for teenagers. Thus confirmation became the standard by which youths were schooled in the way of faith, and the confirmation service retained many of the elements — laying on of hands, anointing with oil, prayers for the receiving of the Holy Spirit — of the original baptismal liturgy (as seen in the story of Lucius).

But with the advent of the Enlightenment, confirmation was viewed in many circles as a particularly pernicious form of indoctrination of the young, because all traditions and symbols were questioned. While confirmation was not abandoned, its importance in the church and the seriousness with which it was taught diminished: "confirmation and catechetical instruction continued to be practiced in the 18th and 19th centuries through the momentum of cultural forces rather than [through] a clear theological understanding of their purpose."[47]

A recovery of the true catechetical purpose of confirmation is one way to respond to the postmodern necessity that our youths learn the language of Christianity.

Confirmation isn't going to be a solution for every youth program, but the following will serve as an example of contextualizing a program to meet a need and fit a place. When I started working at Colonial Church, I inherited a youth ministry that had been in place since 1964 — and a Confirmation program that had been run in the same fashion since 1962. Because it was such an unexamined tradition, Confirmation seemed to be a natural starting place for evaluation.

We put together a task force of pastors, parents, youth committee members, and students to investigate "Confo." We surveyed all the students and their parents who had been through the program over the last five years, and we surveyed the perceptions of the classes coming up in the next five years, all by mail. The results reflected disappointment with the results of Confo, but a general feeling that it was an important program.

The first question the task force tackled was, "Should we have confirmation at Colonial?" The resounding answer was, "Yes!" There are two reasons why that makes sense: One, in the Upper Midwest, confirmation is a part of the cultural landscape — it's up there with learning to drive and moving from middle school to high school. In fact, every year almost half of our incoming

Confo students have no connection to our church. That makes Confo one of our primary *outreach* programs! Many students are pressured by parents or grandparents to get confirmed, even if the family is not churchgoing. So it would seem foolish to euthanize a program that brings 15 to 25 new students to our door every fall.

178

And two, as a Congregational church, confirmation works in the mainline milieu that is our heritage. Even though Colonial leans more toward the evangelical side of the spectrum, Confo began when the church was more on the mainline side, so it has a half century of equity already. We thought that was a solid foundation upon which to build for the future. If we were a Vineyard church in Southern California, however, a confirmation program would probably not be the route to go. All that to say, *every church has to find a regular method to disciple its students appropriate to its local culture, its denominational heritage, and the congregation.*

Further, Confo is simply one in a potpourri of youth ministry programs that includes small groups, large groups, mission and service opportunities, summer camps, retreats, outreach events, et cetera. Confo acts as a primary means of discipling our students, but it's not meant to be the only thing students experience — it's one cog in the machine.

The Next Step

Having decided to continue offering Confo, we next needed to determine what it would look like. Traditionally, Colonial had offered confirmation as a two-year program for eighth and ninth graders — the eighth grade year was optional, and nothing was offered during the summer between the two school years. We discussed offering Confo in sixth grade as students enter middle school, and we considered offering it in 12th grade as a discipleship prep course for the spiritual rigors of college.

There is a future of ministry that is not built around the educational model. There will be an emergence of Christian spiritual development that isn't information-based. I believe that day is upon us. When it's in full bloom, it will put an end to the questions of "What should we do with Confirmation?"

Doug Pagitt

In the end, we decided to offer a "Pastors' Class" – borrowing terminology from our Baptist brothers and sisters – for sixth graders: these students and their parents come to three Monday night classes in September taught by the senior pastor and the youth staff. There they learn about the Ten Commandments, the Lord's Prayer, the Apostles' Creed, and the sacraments, and they are also welcomed into the youth ministry. On the first Sunday of October, World Communion Sunday, the sixth graders are invited to join the congregation at the Lord's Table for their first communion.

Another Pastors' Class is offered to seniors in high school. This is a less formal time of meeting with an assortment of pastors for lunch during the summer after graduation. Topics range from biblical authority to pluralism on college campuses to living a Christian lifestyle.

179

Confirmation itself is for ninth graders (although it's open to older students, too). The Confo journey lasts for one year (actually 14 months). Here's a sketch of that year —

180

• *Orientation and Registration:* In mid-September, we hold a meeting for the new freshmen and their parents on a Wednesday night. As well as laying out the schedule for the whole year, expectations are made clear: attendance will be taken every Wednesday night and students must sign in at worship on Sunday morning; all major events are *required*, not optional; parents *must* accompany their child once a month on Parent Night. (What we have discovered seems counterintuitive in working with adolescents: the higher we raise the standard, the higher the students rise to meet the standard.)

At this gathering meeting, I have a clear message for parents and for students. To the students, I ask: "How many of you *don't* want to be here?" A few always raise their hands. I continue: "I'll tell you what, you come for two months — give me eight Wednesday nights. We'll call it my probation. If, after that, you find Confo to be boring, irrelevant, or otherwise stupid, you don't have to come anymore. Because, you see, it's your parents' job to get you here, and it's my job to keep you here. If you think Confo is dumb after two months, then I'm not doing my job."

And to the parents: "Church has to be a higher priority in most of your families. If your children come here two hours a week and hear me talk about the importance of church participation but the other 166 hours a week they see a model where church always comes *after* hockey, soccer, cheerleading, piano, schoolwork, and sleeping in, then what I say will fall on deaf ears. It's not up to me to disciple your children — it's up to you. I'm just here to help you."

There are several unique hallmarks of Confo —

- *Wednesday Nights:* The Confo class meets every Wednesday evening from 6:45 to 8:00 p.m. The night usually progresses like this: 15 minutes of attendance, goofing around, announcements, and other housekeeping; we often have a student or two get up and tell the class about their band concert or track meet during this time. Then we have 30 minutes of teaching. This is always done in an interactive, dialogical manner. Finally, the students spend the last half an hour in small groups, discussing the night's teaching and anything else they need to talk about.

- *Parent Nights:* Once a month, parents come with their confirmands. On this night the parents are taught the same stuff as the confirmands, and when the students leave for small groups, the parents stay with the youth staff. This affords a rare opportunity: a captive audience of 40 to 60 parents. Here we build community, answer questions, teach, challenge their naiveté about their children, and even gently upbraid them on occasion.

- *Mentors:* Confirmands are placed in groups of two or three and matched with a mentor. Mentors are Christ-centered adults from the congregation who are hand-selected by the youth staff and other pastors. These mentors are trained by the youth staff and others to better understand 14- and 15-year-olds — mainly, they're trained to *listen*. Then they're unleashed to meet with their confirmands as much as they can: breakfast before school, dessert after Confo on Wednesday nights, a bagel after worship on Sunday. Mentors come to Confo once a month and spend the small group time with their confirmands, and they are asked to take their confirmands to a church committee meeting, another style of worship service at another church, a wedding or funeral at Colonial, and a service project.[48]

181

During the year, five significant events mark the progression of the Confo journey —

- *Fall Retreat:* The class and all the leaders head to northern Minnesota on the first weekend of November for a retreat that includes teambuilding exercises, small group formation, teaching on the person of Jesus Christ, and a whole lot of fun.

- *30-Hour Famine:* World Vision's program of fundraising for their worldwide hunger relief efforts has become a huge deal in our church, and the Confo class is the impetus behind it. The students begin raising money in early January. After about six weeks of promotion and fundraising, the Famine weekend is held on the last weekend in February. The confirmands are joined by other youth and by dozens of adults from the congregation for 30 hours of fasting and service work in the community, culminating with a communion service and breakfast meal.

- *Families Moving Forward:* Colonial hosts homeless families four times a year as part of a program that moves them toward apartment rental and self-sufficiency. Confirmands and their mentors volunteer during the F.M.F. week in the spring to cook dinner, clean up, and play with the families' young children.

- *Summer Mission Trip:* The high point of the Confo year is the week we spend doing mission work somewhere in the U.S. Each year it seems there's an overwhelming breakthrough with this group of students who've been together eight or nine months now. The class bonds, they meet physical and spiritual challenges together, and they get a taste of mission work.

- *Confirmation Weekend:* The last Sunday of October is Reformation Sunday, commemorating Martin Luther's 16th-century ecclesiastical revolution. Appropriate to our tradition, this is the day that confirmands are accepted into membership. On Saturday night, we hold a banquet for the students and their parents and a candlelight communion service at which their mentors join them. Then Sunday morning, the confirmands are the center of the worship service: they recite vows that confirm the baptismal vows taken either by their parents or themselves (depending on when they were baptized); the congregation welcomes them into membership; and I pray for each confirmand individually.

The meat of Confo happens every Wednesday night as we try to teach and embody that unique Christian language. Here's an annotated schedule of the year –

- *The Lord's Prayer:* As taught by Jesus at the Sermon on the Mount, this most basic prayer is taught with an eye to exegeting archaic language and bringing out the meaning. After this point, every class closes with a unison recitation of the LP.

- *The Apostles' Creed (The Story of God):* This basic Trinitarian creed is what we say at Colonial every time we celebrate a sacrament. The person of Christ is the primary topic of the Fall Retreat, so the night focusing on the Apostles' Creed deals more on the Father and the Spirit – and particularly the Trinity. (During my first year teaching Confo, a student dropped out after this night, saying he could not profess a belief in the Trinity. I told him I appreciated his integrity. His parents, however, didn't appreciate me very much.) But most importantly, we focus on the Creed as the *story* of our God and his relationship to us.

- *The Story of the Church:* Continuing with the postmodern affinity for *story*, the two thousand year (hi)story of the church is told with stops at Jesus' birth (ca. 4 B.C.), Pentecost (ca. A.D. 29), the Great Schism (1054), Martin Luther (1517), John Calvin (1520), and other interesting personalities and events. The students are brought into the story because it's *their* story, too; they're a part of the story, and the next chapter of the story is going to be written by them!

- *The Story of Congregationalism:* Part of who we are as a church comes from our heritage as people of the Congregational way. As with any denominational story, ours is filled with wonderful high times and embarrassingly sinful foibles, and we let the confirmands in on all the details.

- *The Story of Colonial Church:* On this night we go to the Meetinghouse, where we worship every Sunday, and we revisit how Colonial Church was planted in 1946, how the church has grown and shrunk, the ups and downs of the community's life, and about the different people who've been in leadership. We also talk about how a *meetinghouse* is different than a *sanctuary*, and how the architecture of our worship space reflects who we are as a community of faith. And we invite the students to begin to view Colonial's story as *their* story.

- *The Old Testament:* A brief survey of God's tortured and steadfast relationship with Israel. Plus, the confirmands are taught to distinguish between the literary genres of history, poetry, psalms, proverbs, and prophecy.

- *The New Testament:* In a similar way, the New Testament is brought to life as the story from the time Jesus comes on the scene to the final consummation of Revelation.

- *How to Read the Bible:* We attempt to offer students tools for fruitful Scripture reading. We parse the many different translations available as well as slick packaging techniques aimed to sell them Bibles. We encourage the confirmands to look at the Bible not as a guidebook or rulebook – or even a compendium of theological knowledge – but as the story of God's relationship with humankind.

- *Prayer I:* On this night we discuss different ways to pray and some of the stumbling blocks that keep us from praying. We also wrestle with that most weighty theological question: "Why do we pray?" Answers usually range from "because it works" to "because God wants us to." We even tackle questions about unanswered prayer.

- *Prayer II:* A friend from our church's Intercessors Prayer Group leads the class in a variety of prayers. First, she has everyone in a circle, and each person prays a phrase from one of the Psalms. Then we go to the Meetinghouse for intercessory prayer in small groups. Finally the confirmands come forward one by one to be anointed with oil and for prayer by one of the Intercessors – this sometimes leads to individual words of prophecy to the students, an intense experience that few have before experienced.

- *The Sacraments:* The word *sacrament* in English comes from the word *sacramentum* in Latin, and that is the Latin Vulgate Bible's translation of the Greek word *musterion*. And that word's transliterated as *mystery* in English. Therefore, *sacrament* equals mystery. In other words, the sacraments (in our tradition, baptism and communion) are a mystery – they *cannot* be rationally explained, no matter how hard theologians and youth pastors try. This teaching usually leads to a great discussion among the students regarding their most mysterious experiences involving the sacraments.

- *Baptism:* First we talk about the ancient Jewish tradition of ritual bathings and their symbolism. Then we delve again into the Greek language and the history of *baptizo* in Jesus' day. The synthesis comes when Jesus, as he often does, turns tradition on its head and gives new meaning to an ancient rite. In Jesus' days, Jews washed often to purify themselves – the Essenes would wash their whole bodies six or more times a day. Jesus and his followers practiced *one* baptism and thereby restored the symbolic meaning of the rite. Our discussion usually centers around the infant-adult baptism debate: what did Jesus intend and what was the practice of the early church?

185

The church must be created new, in each generation, not through procreation but through baptism.

Stanley Hauerwas and William H. Willimon, *Resident Aliens: Life in the Christian Colony*, 60

- *Communion:* In order to look at the difference between the three views of this sacrament – Catholic (transubstantiation: the elements change in nature to the body and blood of Christ), Lutheran (consubstantiation: the elements change spiritually but retain their form) and Zwinglian (the Lord's supper is a memorial meal and the elements are symbols) – we look at the three names of this sacrament and their inherent meanings: *Eucharist*, *The Lord's Supper*, and *Communion*.

- *The Meaning of Easter:* Right around Easter – and always on a Parent Night – we tell the story of Jesus' passion from Palm Sunday through Maundy Thursday, and on Good Friday, Holy Saturday and Easter Sunday. Since many of the parents whose children are being confirmed are not churchgoing, this is our surreptitious way of telling them about the saving work of Christ. After the students go to small groups, I spend some time with parents, answering their questions about Jesus and challenging them to live the story themselves.

- *Worship I*: The word *worship* comes from a Middle English word meaning "the state of being worthy of honor." This begs the question, "Is our worship honoring to God?" So we break down Colonial's worship services as a group and try to determine if they honor God and how they could honor God more. As we work through the order of worship, we look at it as a dance in which sometimes God leads and sometimes we lead. We also discuss the meanings of strange words such as *invocation*, *offertory*, and *benediction*.

- *Worship II*: I tell the story of a friend of mine who planted a church in Texas. The elders of this church made shirts that they wear to church occasionally. The shirts read IT'S NOT ABOUT YOU. This gets the Confo class into a great discussion about the meaning and purpose of worship — we even analyze the songs we sing (at the traditional service, the contemporary service, and even at camp) to see if they're more about us or more about God.

- *How to Listen to the Sermon I*: Our senior pastor comes to confirmation and talks to the students about how he puts a sermon together. He explains his narrative/plot approach, comparing it to a movie or sit-com the students are familiar with. The confirmands leave that night with sheets showing that type of narrative progression diagrammed, and they're asked to take notes on Sunday's sermon.

- *How to Listen to the Sermon II*: Our pastor returns to Confo, and the students grill him on the sermon — he also checks to see if they caught the plot hints he hid in the sermon especially for them.

- *The Call to Ministry*: Because I articulated God's call on my life to ministry for the second time when I was in confirmation, I firmly believe that these ninth graders should be asked if they have ever felt an urge toward full-time vocational ministry. The joys and trials of ministry are laid out before them, and in small groups they're asked what would hold them back from entering the ministry.

- *Missions and Outreach*: Our missions and outreach pastor comes to class and talks to the students about why it's so important that Christians and churches be committed to meeting the totality of human need (spiritual, physical, and otherwise) around the world.

- *Church Government and Administration*: Colonial's church business administrator tells the Confo students what she does on a daily basis. She describes how committees work, how the church pays its bills, and how the budget is developed.

186

Interspersed during the year are small group nights, barbeques, and the occasional, out-of-the-blue broomball match at the nearby hockey rink. The schedule is always flexible, and it varies if I'm out of town or if another pastor or a visiting missionary wants to address the class. Special worship services like Ash Wednesday, Maundy Thursday, and Good Friday are also part of our calendar.

187

Tony's teaching outline is fantastic, both for its depth and its breadth. While not all youth workers have the academic background required to teach these subjects, maybe we could read a few books or learn from others so we can develop it. Since students will rarely grow more deeply than the depth of our teaching, it's time we stop playing Marco Polo and splashing around in the shallow end.

Kara Powell

The Result

What we've attempted to do is put together a year of spiritual formation and discipleship for which the level of commitment is high. We've found that the students respond with enthusiasm.

At the end of the year-long journey, the students are asked to write an essay stating why they've chosen to join the congregation in confessing the Apostles' Creed. Here's the text of one of those essays, written by an awesome young woman named Lona:

188

I believe in the Apostle's Creed because it includes the meaning and foundation of the Christian Church. I believe that God has a plan for everybody. It's a comforting thought to know that everything in your life happens for a reason. I think I first began to accept God in my life when we went to Colorado on our mission trip. It became clear to me how he could bring people together to do things they didn't think possible. There were a lot of times that I felt close to God on our trip. One example being when we did our mission projects, or talked to people on the streets. It was one of the few times I had gotten out of my comfort zone and was more than happy that I had. And once I thought about it, going out and talking to people on my own wasn't so bad, because I had God with me, and he wouldn't give me more than I could handle.

I can remember the exact moment that I let him in my life, and accepted the fact that he would love me no matter what. We were at the church service in Denver, listening to testimonies and a choir whose songs are forever burned in my brain. I had been at other services or gatherings where I had held myself back, and didn't let myself cry, and I continued to do the same at this service. I was trying to convince myself that it was stupid, and I wasn't going to be a baby. I was in my own world when I realized I was standing between two people who were on the same level as me, and who had come to be close friends on the trip. We all grabbed each other's hands, and when I looked up, I saw a tear rolling off my neighbor's face. At that moment I knew it was okay to let go, and that I was capable of living a life with God, and I cried more than I ever have. Later, in the Angel's Den, it was even clearer that God wanted us to look to him. He wants us to go to him when we need help.

Building a relationship with him this year has changed my life a lot. The small decisions I make everyday revolve around my religion, and what Jesus would have done if he were in my place. The bigger things, like which people I'm friends with and how I treat people, have come from my relationship with God. Since the beginning of last summer, my whole group of friends has shifted. The decisions they were making weren't

A week after Confirmation Sunday, I received a letter from Lona's dad:

ones I wanted to be a part of if I was going to be close to God, or follow in Jesus' footsteps.

My relationship with God also helps me with everyday things. I pray more now, and it can help me if I'm having a bad day, and can take some weight off my shoulders. While I was backpacking last weekend, I didn't think I was going to make it, and wanted to give up, and just live in the woods. Then I thought about all Jesus had done in his lifetime, and I figured, if he could do that, than I can walk four more miles today. Having him in my life has helped me get my priorities straight. I can think back before confirmation started, and how I wasn't a bit excited. Now I don't know what I would do if he weren't in my life.

No words can adequately express my appreciation. I am sitting at home after one of the most incredible evenings of my life. There was no way of knowing one year ago as Corbin and I sat with our daughters listening to you talk about the upcoming year of confirmation that we would have the experience we had tonight…Lona's transformation this year has been incredible to watch and experience. When you read her paper this evening I could not hold back my tears. Knowing that she has not only accepted Christ into her life, but that Christ has changed her life gives me a great sense of peace.

Testimonies like this are leading me to believe that God still uses an ancient rite like confirmation to dramatically shape students' lives.

Ancient Practices

Across North America, other ancient rites and practices of the church are being rediscovered and applied to youth ministry just as confirmation has been.

Much of the groundbreaking work in this field has been done at the Youth Ministry and Spirituality Project at San Francisco Theological Seminary. The initial thrust there was to follow the progression of 21 youth ministries from 1998 to 2000 as they implemented ancient spiritual practices, first among their leaders and then among their students. The work of the Youth Ministry and Spirituality Project has been very well received, and initial indications are that youth ministries are transformed by this new focus.

We need to be careful to not simply try to revive the faith expressions of the past. Rather we must move from the past — but still fully connected to it — into the future. Youth workers should never settle for simply reliving the past expressions of faith, regardless of how old it is. We need to follow the Christian model and express the God of Abraham, Isaac, Jacob, and Jesus in our day. God allows us to, and the gospel compels us to.

Doug Pagitt

Ancient (and not-so-ancient) authors who are being read by youth and youth pastors include Teresa of Avila, the Desert Fathers, Francis of Assisi, John of the Cross, and John Bunyan. These authors bring alive the truth of Scripture and Christ using mysticism and metaphor – and that's perfectly suited to the postmodern mind.

Among the ancient spiritual practices being used by youth ministries:

- *The Spiritual Exercises of St. Ignatius of Loyola:* Ignatius of Loyola was a rough and ignorant soldier in the 16th century who was dramatically changed by God and went on to found the Jesuit order. The *Exercises* are his reflections on Scripture and his spiritual transformation. Ignatius leads the reader on a four-week path of overcoming one's sin, conforming to the will of Christ, strengthening one's conformation by concentrating on Christ's passion, and transforming the will into love. Many Catholics and Protestants have adapted the Ignatian examination for retreats, small groups, and personal use.[49]

191

- *Lectio Divina:* A major part of the Benedictine Rule of Life, the practice of *lectio divina* can be traced all the way back to the Desert Fathers of the fourth century. The words lectio divina can be translated as "sacred reading" – it is a way to read and pray Scripture that our students have found incredibly meaningful, both in a group and individually. The process is usually fourfold: a short biblical passage is read (three or four times, aloud and slowly), meditated on (listening for a word or phrase that seems to have special urgency), prayed over (asking God for guidance), and contemplated (listening for the intersection of this passage with one's life).[50]

Lectio divina is a great idea, a time-tested format. Teens are attracted to the simplicity of its structure. Some ideas you might try that will deepen the experience and orient it with both past and present: For a preparatory exercise the week before *lectio divina*, teach about the original context and intent of the chosen passage. Paraphrase the Scripture in teams of three to five. Share each group's versions. Talk about why each group chose certain words and images. Share personal stories and experiences that may have influenced each version. During *lectio divina* itself, use a faithful paraphrase of the Scripture passage instead of a traditional translation — Eugene Peterson's *The Message* is a good starting place. During the prayer segment, share specific guidance needs with one other person. Go to candlelighting stations with your prayer partner. As you pray for the other person, light his or her candle — a Christmas Eve, hand-held type.

Sally Morgenthaler

• *The Labyrinth:* The earliest labyrinths were in ancient Egypt. Medieval Christians who couldn't afford to travel to Jerusalem or Rome used labyrinths to take pilgrimages. A labyrinth is not a maze. The most common pattern is the one found on the floor of the cathedral in Chartres, France, with one path to the center and another path back out. The center of the labyrinth represents the New Jerusalem, the heavenly city where Christ will reign at the end of time. Every year we have a local ordained woman bring her 150-foot-radius canvas labyrinth to our youth group and facilitate the experience for our high school students. It is consistently rated one of their favorite times of the year.[51]

192

It's up to Us

If it's true that we're living in a time more like second and third century Rome than like 1950s America, we will do well to learn how Christianity was practiced in ancient days. That's not to say we should become premodern or archaic Christians, but we may have thrown the baby out with the bath water during modern times. Now there is a renewed interest in the spiritual, mystical side of faith, and we have a deep heritage to draw from.

Not much written curriculum exists, however, for those of us wanting to integrate such material into our youth ministries. And if history is any guide, it will be a long time before most youth curriculum publishing companies begin to offer anything like this. So, *it will be up to us to find the ancient source material, adapt it to postmodern times and our own students, and to apply it in our ministries.* Then, it will be up to us to share it.

Take that as a challenge!

193

If what Tony says here is true about the dearth of such curriculum for youths — and I agree — how much more true that there's a dearth for grade schoolers! Our reconsideration of catechesis will force us to go back to the very beginning. That sounds like a lot of work — but what could be more meaningful and exciting? As we deal with postmodernity for adults and youth, we'll be forced to reconsider what and how we teach younger children as well. So...who's going to write *Postmodern Children's Ministry*?

Brian McLaren

the bible 7

While Jesus is the center of our faith, Scripture is the means by which we derive our doctrine and practice. In modern times, the Bible was picked apart, harmonized, abridged, and scientifically scrutinized by various groups. But while our knowledge of Scripture increased, the beauty of the narrative was often lost. Postmodern teenagers want to recover that narrative element and embrace the fact that the Bible is simply God's story – a beautiful compilation of poetry and prose, song and story, diatribe and exhortation, all meant to persuade people to enter the Kingdom of God through Jesus the Christ.

The Bible is propaganda.

In many circles, that sentence might incite a book burning. Before lighting any matches, however, let's unpack the word *propaganda*. Here are some definitions:

1. The systematic propagation of a doctrine or cause or of information reflecting the views and interests of those people advocating such a doctrine or cause.

2. Material disseminated by the advocates of a doctrine or cause: *the selected truths, exaggerations, and lies of wartime propaganda.*

3. A division of the Roman Curia that has authority in the matter of preaching the gospel, of establishing the Church in non-Christian countries, and of administering Church missions in territories where there is no properly organized hierarchy.[52]

196

Is it not true that the Christian Bible is "advocating...a doctrine or cause"? Of course it is! It's advancing the radically wonderful idea that the God who created us loves us so steadfastly that his own Son was sacrificed in order to make that love stick. Propaganda may have negative connotations, but its primary definition applies perfectly to the Bible. (I mean, the Roman Catholic Church calls its mission and church planting branch the Division of Propaganda!)

Being honest about the subjective and persuasive aspects of the Bible with our students – especially our non-Christian students – will greatly benefit our ministries.

But we have not been particularly honest about the Bible in modern times. How the Bible is read and understood, in both more liberal and more conservative circles, has been unduly influenced by modern tendencies. As youth workers, we grew up in churches that were subject to the foundationalist/objectivist Enlightenment paradigm. Although it may seem surprising, *whether we come from a liberal mainline church or a conservative evangelical church, our understanding of Scripture needs to be rethought in a postmodern way*…so that we can move beyond the foundationalism that defined the modern theological project and finally bring the Bible to life for postmodern kids.

The Bible is the nonfiction storybook of God's interaction with his people. It's the lens through which we look at the world — not simply the object we study.

Doug Pagitt

The Modern Liberal Hermeneutic

HERMENEUTIC:
Interpretive; explanatory.

Mainline, liberal churches have grown out of the heritage of people like Friedrich Schleiermacher, who valiantly tried to salvage biblical meaning during the Enlightenment. But in so doing, Schleiermacher and his peers incorporated the truth of Scripture with the new scientific methodology so highly valued by the Western world. Out of this grew the German historical-critical method of the 19th century, which led to the quest for the "truth" behind the narrative of Scripture. Theologian Rudolf Bultmann called this the "kernel of truth" that you find when you strip away the husk of "myth" in any biblical story.

Another outgrowth of this method was the "Quest for the Historical Jesus" that has been going on for 200 years now. We are living with the highly nefarious conclusion of that quest: the Jesus Seminar and its bead polls on what elements of Scripture are *really* real.

The thought was this: there is a universal, human experience of the divine "out there, somewhere," and each religion is an attempt to wrap human arms around God. Many of these theologians believed that Christianity is the best scheme (yet) for accessing the divine, and that individuals in other faiths who are in touch with divine truth are "anonymous Christians." Using scientific methods, they thought, theology can get behind the extraneous traditions to that transcendent truth.

197

In youth ministry, this tradition is represented by churches that proclaim primarily the *teachings* of Jesus and ignore for the most part his miracles and the writings of Paul. While these youth ministries have led the way in things like social justice and service projects, they've often lost touch with the saving work of Christ. There may be an assumption that skeptical teenagers won't believe in a miracle-working savior, but postmodern students *want* a Messiah who has supernatural power!

It seems that in submitting Scripture to modern scientific methodology, the left wing of the western church started down a slippery slope that can culminate only in a highly compromised and truly watered-down Bible.

198

It's very interesting. The modern liberal Christian struggles with inspiration, and yet so many are busy reading *Conversations with God* as if it's inspired! I believe this will prove to be the main issue in the future of the church — our understanding and perspective on the authority of Scripture. In our postmodern world, though, we don't need to argue for the divinity of Christ — that's a given. However, postmoderns don't believe that just because the Bible is supernaturally inspired that it translates to exclusivity — which is what we're really fighting for in the postmodern world. And my fear is that some postmodern teens will become neoliberals and give up the exclusivity of Christ.

What the church lacks most today is strength and the will to fight. My "primary right to never be offended" needs to be examined. The cross *is* an offense! If we seek to make the gospel more palatable or repitch it, we have denied the power of the gospel. That's the only place we have any authority or power — the story of what God has done in Christ. And when we find ways to work around that offense — when we desire safe centers of power rather than oppressed margins — we are no longer Christian.

Jesus and the disciples were killed for telling the truth — and telling the truth is a declaration of war on all other kingdoms.

Mark Driscoll

The Modern Conservative Hermeneutic

But liberals are not alone in accommodating the predominant culture. The right side of the Protestant Christian spectrum — evangelicals and fundamentalists — are also beholden to a foundationalist premise.

Fundamentalism developed as a reaction against the liberal idealism of the Enlightenment, and in so doing established a myopic dogmatism: "The fundamentalists' loyalty to Jesus Christ often implied an uncritical adherence to their own confessions and a censorious stance toward contemporary intellectual challenges." [53] The anti-intellectualism of conservative Christianity has been widely reported and has sometimes resulted in real narrow-mindedness.

For instance, I recently wrote a little piece for *Youthworker* journal on the networking lunch that we have for all the youth workers in our town. The fact that I have lunch with Catholic, Lutheran, and Methodist youth pastors got a couple lines of the essay excerpted and posted on the Web site of a fundamentalist university under the heading, "What in the World Satan Is Up To." It seems these brothers and sisters are so caught up in the bunker mentality of fundamentalism that they cannot imagine God could use nonfundamentalist churches.

The weakness of fundamentalism is its reliance on a biblical-doctrinal foundationalism (see Chapter 1). By defining themselves over against culture, fundamentalists are being defined by culture — the very thing they repudiate. What's more, they are using a modern scheme — foundationalism — to do it. Therefore, the continuing revelation of God in nature and humanity is not allowed.

Scripture speaks plainly of continuing revelation. In John 14:26, Jesus says that the Spirit "will teach you all things and will remind you of everything." And the author of Hebrews proclaims that "the word of God is living" (4:12). Finally, remember that there was no Bible for the first four centuries of the church, and God was clearly active during that period of history.

199

Evangelicalism grew out of a more moderate stance that attempted to balance reason and revelation:

> The original evangelical strategy for bringing the gospel to America by emphasizing the commonality between reason and revelation has resulted in the accolades that it currently enjoys. But has this strategy actually worked to subvert the mission? [Has] evangelicalism's confidence in reason and delight with American culture become its quagmire? So it seems. Fifty years later the question no longer concerns the trivialization of reason but the trivialization of revelation! This concern is crucial. [54]

200

In other words, in the rush to win the world's intellectual appreciation, the evangelical church gave away too much. What was unique about evangelicalism was adjusted to accommodate Western culture — getting on TV, getting tenure on university faculties, and getting "believing" politicians elected. Because they were secularized by their popularity, biblical truths were watered down or lost.

Evangelicals and fundamentalists both got bogged down, too, in the quest to prove the factual basis of Scripture. Gallons of ink have been spilled trying to "prove" that Jonah could really be swallowed by a fish or that the whole earth really was flooded or that the world was created in seven 24-hour days or that Jesus really rose from the dead (yes, he did, but just try and prove that scientifically…you can't!).

You will never be able to prove — even to yourself — that Jesus exists. Belief must be an inner experience. As long you try to prove the object of your belief intellectually, your efforts will stand in the way of such an experience.

J. Heinrich Arnold, *Discipleship*, 26

So, ironically, liberals and conservatives fell into the same modern trap: "Whether meaning was found in eternal truths that the text symbolized (as for liberals) or identified exclusively with the story's factual reference (as for conservatives), both displaced the priority of Scripture."[55]

Beyond Liberalism and Fundamentalism[56]

We are dealing with postmodern students who are going to take what we teach them to postmodern universities (the very heart of the postmodern revolution) and into an increasingly postmodern world. We had better rethink how we understand the Bible!

The first order of business is to admit that our cultural context colors the way we read Scripture. We read the Bible through lenses that are fashioned by our surroundings, and to try and say that we come to the text objectively is self-deceptive. A white, suburban, 13-year-old male is going to read a passage much differently than a black, urban, 17-year-old female. This is one of the reasons why so may of our teens are bored by the worship in our churches — and why many churches are starting youth worship and church-within-a-church programs: when preachers are preparing sermons, they are most cognizant of what the text has to say to the *adults* of their congregations. The fact is, that text may say something very different to the high school students of the church.

For instance, Jesus' brief conversation with the rich young ruler (Luke 18:18-27) is a very poignant story for the rich young students with whom I work. It would take a lot more work for a youth pastor in a underprivileged environment to bring that story to life, however. But that youth pastor can more easily access the Beatitudes from the Sermon on the Mount, whereas those blessings often seem a long way from the day-to-day experiences of my affluent students.

So we must stop looking for some objective Truth that is available when we delve into the text of the Bible — remember, "the word of God is living and active" (Hebrews 4:12). Jesus says, "I am the way, and the truth, and the life. No one comes to the Father except through me." That is truth. But what that means to a student who's struggling to overcome a drug addiction — *how* Jesus is "the truth" — will necessarily be different than what it means to the student who's the captain of the basketball team and seems to have it all together. Jesus is the truth for both students, but he looks very different to each. As their youth workers, *let's embrace that truth as each student comes to it, without imposing our own slanted view of biblical truth on them.* That's not to say that there are no standards, but we probably need to widen our parentheses of scriptural orthodoxy.

201

What Tony says here about truth and objectivity is very clear, very important, and very radical. I often hear Christians beating the drum of "Absolute truth! Absolute truth!" and I wonder if they know what they're against (relativism, nihilism, hedonism) or in favor of. Are they for this myth of objectivism — an Enlightenment ideal that's not a biblical category? Are they for absolute knowledge — the idea that humans are capable (with or without the Bible) of absolute, bulletproof, undoubtable, inerrant knowledge (even though the Bible itself says, "we know in part")? Our brethren would do well to ponder these paragraphs and let themselves get rocked and unsettled for a while.

Brian McLaren

Propaganda

The second order of business is to come to terms with the fact that the Bible is propaganda. Just as we do not read the Bible from a neutral, objective place, it was not written as a neutral, objective book.

This whole concept of neutral, objective writing is a modern construction anyway. When Herodotus wrote the first "history" in about 445 B.C., he was accused almost immediately of bias in his reporting – he has thus been called both the "Father of History" *and* the "Father of Lies." And it was assumed that later historians were simply singing the praises of one leader or another, one administration or another, one family or another in their writings.

202

For centuries prior to our Modern Era, the church viewed the gospel as a Romance, a cosmic drama whose themes permeated our own stories and drew together all the random scenes in a redemptive wholeness. But our rationalistic approach to life, which has dominated Western culture for hundreds of years, has stripped us of that, leaving a faith that is barely more than mere fact-telling. Modern evangelicalism reads like an IRS 1040 form: It's true, all the data is there, but it doesn't take your breath away.

Brent Curtis and John Eldredge, *The Sacred Romance*, 45

It has only been since the Enlightenment that historians and reporters have propagated the lie that they are composing the true, factual, neutral, and objective account of an event or a person. But really, do you think that an American high school textbook has the same account of Pearl Harbor as a Japanese high school textbook? Surely not. Which is "more accurate"? Well, that event looks very different depending which side of the Pacific Ocean you come from – so each textbook has "truth." The same might be said of the Battle of Wounded Knee as told by a relative of an American soldier versus the version told by the relative of a Lakota. "Truth" is a slippery thing to pin down. "Objective Truth" simply doesn't exist to the postmodern.

So the Gospel writers were recording their accounts in a milieu that accepted and understood their subjectivity – their audience *expected* them to be out to prove a point. Each Gospel writer had a distinct audience, so each Gospel has a different shading – but each was out to advocate the position that Jesus of Nazareth is the Christ.

203

This is a modern imposition on a biblical mindset. The Gospel writers were not focused on making an academic case or solving the problem of who Jesus was. They were out to convey a message about the mystery of God being revealed in human form and inviting people to experience the mystery they were a part of. You *figure out* a puzzle, you *solve* a problem, but you *kneel* in a mystery. That's why ministry in the 21st century is the very similar to ministry in the first century — there's a profound openness in postmodern culture to the mystery of the Christian faith and the wonder of the everyday. Postmoderns don't approach life as a problem to be solved but a mystery to be experienced and lived.

Leonard Sweet

Some of us might be tempted to take the tack with our students that the Bible is one big proof text for the divinity of Jesus. But the writers of the New Testament already believed that, and they are attempting to convince everyone else that their viewpoint is right. That makes the Bible more like a political treatise than a history textbook. Students who have little or no experience with the Bible will greatly benefit if, when we introduce them to it, we set it up as a compilation of books that attempt to convince them of something. That way, the students know what they're dealing with.

Further, the meaning of Scripture is very much influenced by our church communities. We didn't find the Bible in a cave somewhere – it's been with us for almost 2,000 years. And Christians have been debating the meanings of words, phrases, and concepts therein ever since. The church believes and teaches that this compendium of books is somehow mystically and miraculously inspired, the authoritative word of God. Although this is the truth we proclaim, it does not seem particularly objective to someone who is not a Christian. In fact, we're not being objective about the Bible, because we believe that it's God's Word. So why act as though we are objective, neutral scientists in approaching this book? The fact is, we love it, we believe what it says, and we find God in its pages. We can be unashamed of our bias for the Bible!

Another thing that students need to hear from us, whether we're giving a talk or leading a Bible study, is that we bring *one point of view* on this passage, and another youth pastor down the road might bring a different but equally valid interpretation. (Just think how the Baptist and Catholic youth pastors might differently teach Matthew 16:17-19 where Jesus gives Peter the keys to the church…)

Recovering Narrative

The Bible was written by dozens of authors over three millennia. And when these diverse, eclectic books are gathered together, they *tell a story*. We may have fallen into another trap of late when we've tried to make the Bible into a systematic theology. Books abound on "Promises of the Bible" and "Bible Lists," but Scripture was given to us by God in this form for a reason: it tells the "old, old story of Jesus and his love." To refashion the Bible into lists and charts is to separate from their contexts passages that are meant to be part of a song in the Psalms or part of a bigger argument in Romans or part of a hymn in 1 John. Let's teach our students whole books of the Bible instead of verses here and there.

And let's teach them the whole story of Scripture by *telling them stories*. Much has been said about our world's lack of oral tradition. In generations past, people could tell stories that would last hours. In ancient Greece, it took two 12-hour sessions to sing the whole *Iliad*, and the singers had it memorized word for word! Those days are gone for good, but we can recover some of that sense of story with our students — we have a compilation of the best stories ever written down, after all — not to mention songs, wise sayings, prophecies, theological treatises, and a really freaky book at the end.

205

As the ultimate author of Scripture, God is more like an artist than a photographer.

George Hunsinger, "What Can Evangelicals & Postliberals Learn from Each Other? The Carl Henry-Hans Frei Exchange Reconsidered" in Timothy R. Philips and Dennis L. Okham, eds., *The Nature of Confession*, 146

Think of a time when you heard a preacher or youth pastor or speaker really bring to life a biblical story. Wasn't it an awesome experience? Didn't you feel transported into the midst of the story? Try it. Or try an even harder practice: give a first-person talk, where you are one of the characters in the story — you can be a major player (Peter, Mary, Martha, Thomas), or you can make up a fictional character who's on the periphery, watching biblical events unfold.

206

I totally agree with Tony. There's nothing like watching teens respond to stories when we tell them with life and color. But I also believe that we need to do more. What we need in our stories is solid theology — even systematic theology! We can help reshape the worldviews of postmodern youths so they are thoroughly biblical. We should be doing a lot of what I call "theo-topical" preaching — where the messages are designed to help shape kids' theological grids and force them to think. I'm not, however, talking about theology that feels like a math equation or is illustrated by end-times charts or fruitless arguments about when the Rapture will occur. I'm talking about going back to the basic historical doctrines of the faith — the Trinity, the deity of Christ, the origin of man, sin, et cetera. Postmodern teens are starving for this.

Dan Kimball

There may not be a better line for us to add to our job descriptions or résumés: "Youth pastor: brings the Bible to life for students." We should make the telling of biblical narrative primary to our personal ministries.

If our job is to "bring the Bible to life," that implies the Bible is somehow already (at least partly) dead. That's poor theology, if not heresy! The Bible *is* alive; we don't have to make it so. Our job is to present its historical and cultural contexts so that its *inherent* life shines forth to our students.

Kara Powell

The Death of the Metanarrative?

This is one area in which we will be breaking dramatically with postmodern philosophy. A "metanarrative" is a story that is universally applicable and acceptable to all human beings. Just such a story has been the quest of all religions, according to many people. Postmodern philosophers, namely Jean-François Lyotard, have declared that there is no such thing as an all-encompassing story, that there's only an assortment of local, micronarratives.

207

To make postmodernity

a censor of the Great
Story that both Scripture

208

and tradition have told is

to enter the familiar land

of Babylonian captivity.

Gabriel Fackre, "Narrative: Evangelical, Postliberal, Ecumenical" in Timothy R. Philips and Dennis L. Okham, eds., *The Nature of Confession*, 124

As Christians, of course, we believe that there is, indeed, one story into which all humanity and the entire cosmos can be enfolded. It's the story that begins with God and only God, and continues through his creation, the irresistibility of sin for the first humans, the covenants of the Old Testament, the life, death, and resurrection of Jesus Christ, and the birth of the church. In fact, we even know how this story will end — with a trumpet blast on the last day and a new heaven and new earth before our eyes.

Although I fully agree with Tony that for Christians there is a meta-narrative, I also sympathize with postmodern skepticism. I'm not so confident that any of us really understands that metanarrative very well. In other words, I know that God's metanarrative is true, complete, and perfect; on the other hand, your version of it, or mine, or even Billy Graham's, is certainly partial, more or less distorted, and less than perfect. This means, I believe, that while we ought to proclaim our understanding of the Grand Story with confidence (because we dare not underestimate God's capacity to work through our proclamation, even though it is flawed), we also should do so with humility (because we dare not underestimate our capacity to be mistaken).

Brian McLaren

This is no small story. This is a grand, sweeping metanarrative — it describes all, contains all, and answers all.

But to a world that doesn't believe that such a metanarrative exists, we are going to have to be creative in how we tell the story. Instead of getting a student to profess a belief in the authority of Scripture on the front end, we may be better off first inviting students into the community, to experience the truth of Scripture as it's lived out by Christian students and leaders. As pre-Christian students experience biblical love, and as they're exposed to the stories of Scripture, the Bible will begin to take on "truth value" for them. And, after some time, as they find themselves folded into the story of Abraham and Sarah, Jacob and Ruth, Paul and Lydia, they will find the Bible is indeed a metanarrative into which every human being's story is written.

209

Renewing Biblical Literacy

Another positive consequence of recovering the story of Scripture is that we will be teaching students the basis for most of Western literature.

210

We are in a postmodern age. Authors steeped in the Bible are diminishing in number, and one cannot help but wonder about the future of Western literary tradition. But it would be wrong to think of this only as a literary problem. If imagination is basic to thought then the weakening of the biblical substructure of our culture's communal imagination may dry up the wellsprings of Western humanistic creativity in general.

George A. Lindbeck, "The Church's Mission to a Postmodern
Culture" in Frederic B. Burnham, ed., *Postmodern Theology:
Christian Faith in a Pluralist World*, 47

In years past, even the most anti-Christian Enlightenment philosophers were more versed in the Old and New Testaments than many pastors are today. Much has been said and written about the Bible being the primary text of study at universities like Harvard and Yale 200 years ago.

Times have changed – necessarily so. But as Lindbeck argues, "There is a sense in which most of Western literature is midrashic commentary" on the Bible.[57] For someone familiar with the stories of the Bible, the scriptural allusions in *Moby Dick, The Brothers Karamazov,* or *The Red Badge of Courage* may seem obvious. But we are in times when much of that biblical literacy has been lost – so much so that a movie like *The Matrix,* in which the scriptural imagery just about pummels you over the head, slips past many critics and viewers without a word about the symbolism.

The Bible, with its stories of good and evil, its romance, its poetry, its death and destruction, and its science fiction, is not only rife with ideas for screenplays, it needs to be the basis of the moral imagination of our youth. Centuries ago, John Calvin said that Scripture should be the lens through which we see the world. Indeed, Scripture was long the common tongue of half of the world. With its cultural demotion, our ability to communicate has been diminished. With its recovery, the students with whom we work can revitalize and ennoble the currently banal level of cultural conversation.

That is to say, this generation of students has the ability to breathe new life into our sacred text, particularly because postmodernism has influenced many people to be more open to the biblical narrative. They may be able to bring the Bible back to the level of *the* metanarrative by which human beings determine how to live their lives, how to talk about politics, science, and relationships, and how to make decisions.

211

212

This will not, however, come about with memorization of individual Scripture verses, violently ripped out of the God-given contexts. "Rather it is the patterns and details of its sagas and stories, its images and symbols, its syntax and grammar, which need to be internalized if one is to think scripturally…What are to be promoted are those approaches that increase familiarity with the actual text."[58]

If our youth have a hankering to memorize, we should help them memorize a whole psalm, or a chapter of Ephesians, or the Sermon on the Mount. I once heard a former monk say the best thing about being a monk was memorizing all 150 psalms – now *there's* a goal to shoot for!

Nor will our students learn to inhabit the biblical narrative and make it their own if we pull single verses out of their contexts and proof-text them to suit our own theological ends. When giving a talk, we must use whole paragraphs or chapters of Scripture, we must set up the text we are using by setting the scene and describing the context. Only then are we bringing the scriptural narrative to life with integrity.

The Jesus Journey

In order to revive the Bible for postmodern generations, we must be very creative in our approach.

Mark Miller, a youth pastor in Ohio, has developed a postmodern exemplar he calls The Jesus Journey. A group of high school students go on a weekend retreat, and over the course of the weekend, they *experience* the entirety of the Bible. They journey from Genesis through Revelation over two and a half days through music, video, silence, light, darkness, and other stimuli. Mark and his staff construct an atmosphere that brings the Bible to life.

213

There are no talks, no explanations. The youth pastor never gets up to tell the kids what the Bible *really means*. Instead, Mark trusts God enough to let Scripture speak for itself. And the result has been amazing: his students have seen the Bible in a new light, as a living, breathing story that envelops them. It's not their parents' Bible anymore — it becomes *theirs*, it becomes *their story*, and they will never read the Bible the same way again.

We all need to be as creative with God's Word as Mark is, because God has given us a compendium of texts that run the gamut. If God was so imaginative in his creation of Scripture, our duty is to be similarly creative in our presentation of it to our students. Let your mind simmer — what could you do with the book of Job? Or with a psalm? Or, to really think outside the box, with Revelation?

In the end, we do God dishonor when we offer the Bible to kids in stale, time-worn ways, and we do him honor when we look at our postmodern students and ask ourselves, "How can I bring God's word to life for them?"

toward a holistic practice of youth ministry

Many postmodern philosophers and theologians have challenged us to rearrange our priorities of thought and to put ethics (both personal and communal) first. This charge is especially important for youth workers to consider: young souls are entrusted to our care, so our personal ethics are paramount. We'll do well to examine how we live, what we value, and how we can develop holistically — so we can help our students do the same.

8

Not long ago, I spent some time with a couple of youth ministry veterans. We got to talking about "the biggest change in youth ministry," and we quickly reached a consensus: *professionalization*. Even 30 years ago, there was no such thing as a "youth ministry veteran."

In the last couple decades though, thousands of men and women have gone into professional youth ministry, and thousands of churches have hired us. While the history of youth ministry stretches back a century or so, only very recently have Christian colleges and seminaries offered classes and majors in youth ministry. Support organizations and parachurch ministries related to youth work have also blossomed since the 1960s.

216

For the most part, this has been a good thing. Those of us in youth ministry feel support, we have conferences and conventions to attend, and we have books written exclusively for us. But we must not lose sight of how new all this professionalism really is. Colleges and seminaries struggle with what classes to offer in the field of youth ministry, and they wonder whom to hire to teach the classes – there aren't many individuals out there with Ph.D.s in youth ministry.

Some of us may even struggle with putting together job descriptions or résumés. Are we supposed to be program directors or pastors or spiritual directors or counselors or administrators or trainers? Or, worse yet, all of the above? In some ways, we are like computer programmers: our jobs didn't exist 50 years ago, and they're evolving at a very rapid pace. In another way, though, our jobs are very different: most computer programmers show up at work each day with a very concrete list of what needs to be done, whereas in the youth ministry world, anything can happen!

I am fascinated by Tony's description of the youth ministry profession and feel — in light of the importance of this dynamic period of life we call "youth" — that youth ministry is tremendously undervalued. I wonder if we should go back to a more ancient idea...that people become young adults at puberty. In that case, youth ministry is really ministry to adults. It's adult pastoral work — nothing less. And pastoral work at a critically important, pivotal, dynamic, and exciting period of adulthood — young adulthood.

Brian McLaren

So there is a need for us to develop a picture of what it means to be a youth pastor – what does this strange calling really entail? For guidance, we can look to Alasdair MacIntyre.

After Virtue

By many accounts, the most significant book on ethics written in the 20th century is MacIntyre's *After Virtue*. Written in 1981 and revised in 1984, it's a work that took the postmodernism of many academic fields and applied it to all of life. Although MacIntyre writes about moral reasoning, he provides tools that are critical to the evaluation of many fields, youth ministry included, because he offers a holistic alternative to counter modernity's fragmentation.

217

MacIntyre begins by recounting the failure of the Enlightenment. The first problem of the Enlightenment philosophers was that they rejected the Judeo-Christian *telos* (the Greek word for *end*) of human existence. Whereas the goal of human life had been generally agreed upon (e.g., "What is the chief end of man? To glorify God and enjoy him forever."), the goal of the moral life became vacuous during the Enlightenment – because there is no goal without God in the mix! For the first time, Western civilization could not come to consensus on the question, "What is the meaning of life?"

We see this in values-based curriculum in the public schools. When speakers come in and lead assemblies and retreats, they teach students about the values of the school: honesty, respect, truth, courage, teamwork. The problem comes with the "why" questions: *Why* should a student be honest at school? The answers fall short: because that's the only way the school will function properly; because you want others to be honest with you, et cetera. The goals toward which honesty propels students are unsatisfactory.

MacIntyre responds to this goalless existence by writing, "To know oneself as…a social person is however not to occupy a static and fixed position. It is to find oneself placed at a certain point on a journey with set goals; to move through life is to make progress – or to fail to make progress – toward a given end."[59] In order to live a life of moral discipline, a person must have a goal that's the impetus for such discipline.

Without an end, the theories of moral and ethical behavior went in several different directions during and after the Enlightenment. Utilitarian theory, for instance, teaches that what is good for the many outweighs what is good for the few. Professor Peter Singer of Princeton University has used this theory to propose that parents can kill their disabled children within the first 28 days of life because of the toll these children take on society.

Then there's social contract theory, which advocates natural human rights. This is what influenced the founders of the United States and those who wrote the Declaration of Independence and the Constitution. The problem is that inalienable rights were make believe, invented by men like John Locke and Thomas Jefferson: "there are no such rights, and belief in them is one with belief in witches and unicorns…every attempt to give good reasons for believing that there *are* such rights has failed."[60]

We have inherited these and other theories regarding how human beings should coexist on this planet. The problem is that we have inherited only fragments of each, and we do not agree on which theory to use. This is why, MacIntyre writes, abortion opponents and abortion advocates stand on either side of a street and scream at each other: both use incomplete theories, and both play by rules the other hasn't agreed to. When a culturally agreed upon way to converse about moral issues is lacking, all argument collapses into emotion.

This fragmentation is seen throughout the Western world, and it's not restricted to moral reasoning. Religious faith is another area in which many (if not most) people do not follow one comprehensive and coherent system but syncretize beliefs from many different traditions. This is why faithful churchgoing people may feel no inner dissonance in reading New Age books like *The Celestine Prophecy* and *Embraced by the Light* and adding the "truths" of these books to their spiritual grab bags. Instead of adhering to one, orthodox belief structure (or web), many people compile an assortment of fragments they pick up hither and thither. And the current information revolution is only making this problem more acute.

218

MacIntyre's Corrective

What MacIntyre proposes in response to post-Enlightenment fragmentation is an updated version of Aristotle's ethics. Aristotle wrote that human beings must exhibit certain virtues in order to work toward the goal of life. MacIntyre takes one step back and says that before virtues come practices. He defines them as –

> any coherent and complex form of socially established cooperative human activity through which the goods internal to that form of activity are realized in the course of trying to achieve those standards of excellence which are appropriate to, and partially definitive of, that form of activity, with the result that human powers to achieve excellence, and human conceptions of the ends and goods involved, are systematically extended.[61]

219

He goes on to write that playing football is a practice, but throwing a football is not; architecture is a practice, but bricklaying is not. *Youth ministry is a practice*, but leading a small group is not. A practice is a holistic endeavor that is undertaken with a goal in mind, and each practice has internal and external goods that come when it is practiced well. These "goods" are to be understood as the product of the practice, though not in a moral sense.

Then MacIntyre goes on to suggest that inherent in any practice is a group of virtues necessary for that practice. When these virtues are mastered, the practice is perfected, and progress is made toward the goal –

220

> The virtues therefore are to be understood as those dispositions which will not only sustain practices and enable us to achieve the goods internal to practices, but which will also sustain us in the relevant kind of quest for the good, by enabling us to overcome the harms, dangers, temptations and distractions which we encounter, and which will furnish us with increasing self-knowledge and increasing knowledge of the good.[62]

What virtues are necessary for a practice – and how a practice is best pursued – are determined by a community over time and are handed down by way of tradition. This will raise a little bit of a dilemma for youth ministry, since it is such a new practice.

MacIntyre has proposed a remedy for the fragmentation of modernism, a holistic tradition of practices and virtues, all of which are directed at a goal.

The *Telos* of Youth Ministry

Because we are Christians, determining the goal of our lives as youth pastors is not difficult. Already quoted above was the first question and answer from the Westminster Catechism: "What is the chief end of man? To glorify God and enjoy him forever." To this could be added any number of scriptural citations. We love God with all our heart, soul, and mind (Matthew 22:37; Mark 12:30; Luke 10:27). We "all reach unity in the faith and in the knowledge of the Son of God and become mature, attaining to the whole measure of the fullness of Christ" (Ephesians 4:13). We are conformed to the image of Christ (Romans 8:29).

221

Think of it. What if everything we did as youth workers was focused on the goal that we might be conformed to Christ's image! No more measurements based on numbers or size of budget or staff. At our annual review, the senior pastor would ask, "Are you and your students being conformed to the image of Christ?"

The recent push to be "purpose driven" is a step in the right direction, for it has challenged us to ask why we do what we do. But before we write purpose, vision, and mission statements, maybe we should write *Telos* Statements – our lives as youth pastors would be ordered by that ultimate goal. An agreed upon end, or goal, for the individual Christian, or for the church community, would also be an excellent way to order a church staff and an entire congregation.

222

The reality is that postmoderns dislike all kinds of measurement — and yet built into the very fabric of just about every church is the process of measurement. Institutions simply can't function without counting, comparing, listing, evaluating. So, ministering to postmoderns requires more than a new way of doing ministry, it requires merely a new way of thinking. Ministering to postmoderns doesn't merely require some adjustments, it requires a dismantling of the system! The issue is not what kind of purpose statements should we write, it's how can we learn to live without *any* purpose statements? This generation is perfectly happy just *experiencing* Jesus. The worst thing we can do is give the impression that the goal of the Christian life is to experience more of Jesus tomorrow. No. The postmodern says, "I don't want more of Jesus; I'm satisfied with however much of Jesus I experience today."

Mike Yaconelli

The Practice of Youth Ministry

The profession of youth ministry is an amalgam of the fragments from several other practices, but it's so new that there are very few long-standing and time-tested traditions. Our profession has been influenced by many other professions: pastoral minister, camp director, social worker, therapist, program director, preacher, evangelist, and many others. A youth pastor is trying to perform a compilation of all these roles, and only fragments of each. Members of the congregation and other pastoral staff, meanwhile, have little or no idea what a youth pastor really is or does. One family wants you to be a social worker, another wants a spiritual guide; the committee wants a program director, and the senior pastor wants an evangelist.

Many of us are not trained in any of these fields, or only in one or two. Full-time, professional youth workers run the gamut in education from a high school education to two years of Bible college to a college degree to a Masters in Christian Education or Divinity to a Ph.D. What other profession boasts members with such a wide array of training – and all expected to do basically the same thing? To remedy this, more institutions are offering degrees and certificates in youth ministry, but the lack of unity is indicative of the fragmentation of our profession.

So we bring to the job of youth ministry fragmented experience, fragmented education, and fragmented expectations. To view youth ministry as a practice will bring much needed holism to our vocation.

223

A practice is a "coherent and complex form of socially established cooperative human activity." There is little doubt that youth ministry is complex – as we have seen it is a strange hybrid that requires many different skill sets for competence. Coherence, however, is noticeably lacking. Very few churches or senior pastors can even articulate why they want a youth pastor on staff – they have one of us because it seems like the right thing to do. *Therefore, it is up to us to gather our resources across North America and begin to articulate a unified and holistic vision of the practice of youth ministry.*

Sure. But we could also conclude that youth ministry is itself a construct of modernity, and as such, should be abandoned along with so many other things as a bad idea. Can we really say hand-on-heart that we would not advocate this if it were not for our careers, businesses, institutions, and interests?

Pete Ward

224

To begin, we might look at the internal goods of youth ministry — those results or effects that are inherent even to the practice of our profession. For instance, when youth ministry is practiced to a "standard of excellence," youth pastors become more holy, better listeners, humble, sincere, and disciplined. In short, an "internal good" of youth ministry is that, when we do it well, we become better disciples of Christ.

The "external goods" of youth ministry are those benefits outside of us that blossom when the same standards of excellence are met. To begin that list, we might say that students meet and fall in love with Christ; students become disciples; students find a safe place to work through their problems; students worship God; and churches grow. All these goods internal and external to our vocation are, of course, by the grace of God, but it is only by measuring the internal and external good of our youth ministry that we can get a sense of our success. When the afore-mentioned progress is happening, we're in line with our *telos*.

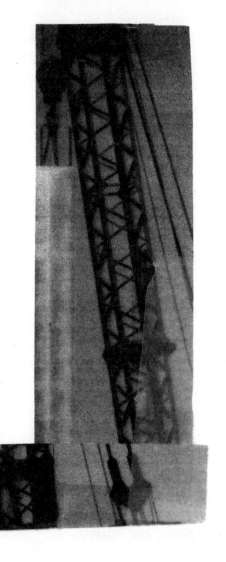

The Virtues Required for Youth Ministry

The next step in MacIntyre's process for developing a holistic approach to the practice of youth ministry is to reflect on what virtues are necessary to help us achieve the best in youth ministry — and to avoid the pitfalls and temptations. A good place to begin, of course, is with Scripture. Paul writes that the fruits of the Spirit are "love, joy, peace, patience, kindness, goodness, faithfulness, gentleness and self-control" (Galatians 5:22-23). These are virtues universal to disciples of Christ, and they are especially applicable to leaders in the church.

Beyond biblical virtues, others seem to be particularly essential for youth workers. One is *maturity*. Think of the number of times each of us is entrusted by parents with their children. It would seem there's a reason that most people are 35 or 40 before they have a 15-year-old — they've got that much more life experience to draw upon in raising children. Twenty five- and 30-year-old youth workers, on the other hand, are often given responsibility over a dozen teenage students, sometimes taking them across the country or around the world! Making wise decisions with a group of students while doing mission work in the barrios of Mexico City takes people with maturity beyond their years.

Another necessary virtue is *political savvy*. In order to negotiate the rough seas of church politics, youth pastors need to exercise a lot of moxie when dealing with outraged parents, demanding committees, unsupportive pastors, and difficult students. Many youth workers have lost their jobs due to their inability to massage politically delicate situations in their churches. This is a particularly difficult virtue to develop, too, because youth pastors usually have little political clout to wield and few advocates in powerful positions. It's needed because youth workers stand at the lower end of the church totem pole, yet are expected to be the biggest risk-takers on staff!

225

Youth ministers must have the *ability to communicate*. This world is filled with sincere, faithful Christians who are particularly skilled at communication, and for teenagers, communication is essential — in many ways they're just entering the world of mature, adult communication. So to match youths with youth workers who have difficulty communicating is never a good idea. Communicating the gospel, however, can happen in various and complementary ways. Some youth workers may be better at speaking in front of a group (although this type of communication is waning in the postmodern world), others are better at leading discussions, and still others work better one-on-one. No matter the method, the ability to communicate and teach the truth of the gospel to youths, particularly in innovative ways, is essential.

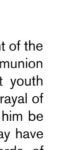

Youth pastors necessarily must be a *people of prayer*. The weight of the task of youth ministry simply must be alleviated by constant communion with the God who's called us into this vocation. To attempt youth ministry alone, without the benefit of God's partnership, is a betrayal of the call. He only wants us in this ministry if we're willing to let him be our partner. Youth workers who are too arrogant or busy to pray have no place in youth work, and their work won't meet standards of excellence over the long haul.

226

Leadership is another necessary virtue. Particularly in an age when large group speaking is out and small groups and one-on-one time is in, youth pastors cannot truly build relationships with more than about a dozen kids. This necessitates teams of volunteer leaders that shepherd their own groups of students, or even mentor individual students. For this to happen, volunteer leaders must have respect for the youth pastors, and the youth pastors must be able to lead the volunteers — to train, teach, correct, and appreciate them. Without the ability to lead — out of humility and calling, not arrogance — only a very small group of students will be reached.

The preceding is only a beginning list of virtues necessary for excellent youth ministry. To this list might be added *teamwork, listening, boundaries*, and more. In all cases, the virtues are more like fruits of the Spirit than gifts of the Spirit — some come more easily to some individuals than others — but all can be learned and developed over time, with practice, effort, and discipline.

Again, we need to start conversations in churches, colleges, and seminaries — yes, in our networks, our denominations, and our conventions — about the list of virtues necessary for the practice of excellent youth ministry. This will help church search committees as they look to hire youth staff. It will help individuals as they attempt to discern whether or not God has called them into youth ministry. And it will help those of us in youth ministry as we mentor our interns and the new youth worker who just arrived at the church down the street.

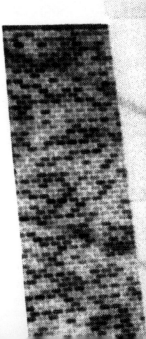

Tony brings up a great point regarding the need to be politically savvy in our churches. As we youth workers present postmodern perspectives to our senior pastors, it probably will seem very strange and foreign to them — even scary! Postmodernism can lead to conflicts and misunderstandings. So it's critical that we educate our senior pastors and others on our church staffs about this cultural shift happening around them. Maybe they could dig into this book — or perhaps articles or audio tapes will help. Whatever method you choose, don't shy away from discussing postmodernism with them — or else you'll only find yourself isolated. This is new territory we're entering, and you can't go there alone.

Dan Kimball

227

A Holistic Life

The most pressing need for youth workers in the postmodern context is to develop a holistic rule of life. In an age when the gospel message is needed more than ever – and the media available to communicate it is so rapidly expanding – the temptation is to do more, more, and still more. More events. More programs. More kids coming to Christ. But the answer for us is just the opposite. Instead of speeding up, we need to slow down. Instead of casting the net wider, we must focus on the few.

228

A long-time youth worker who used to have a huge group on Sunday nights, sometimes 300 students, has seen it shrink to about 40 very committed student disciples. When asked how many committed disciples he had back in the day of his big numbers, he said, "About 40." His church, it seems, is able to handle discipling about that many students. That is not to say that God will not grow that number, but it has served to take the pressure off this youth pastor to have big numbers all the time.

Postmodern kids need to see examples of adults who have boundaries. They've looked at their parents' pursuit of wealth, and they're disgusted – and yet they're the most consumeristic teens of all time. Our witness to them should reach beyond words. It should include healthy families, strong friendships, and spiritual disciplines. A youth pastor's life should include hobbies that have nothing to do with ministry. We'd do well to set an example as those who've stepped out of the rat race, those who don't spend all our money on the brand *du jour*, those who have unplugged our TVs.

Yes. Teens need to be in relationship with mature adults who have boundaries, wisdom, and self-discipline. Modeling a behavior is worth 10 books on the subject. That said, we have to face the reality that, more than we might assume, the mature adults they need in their lives may not be their parents. And youth workers alone aren't going to be enough. How are we going to expand the "mentoring" options? Can we start involving more adults than just "sponsor couples" in our car washes and feeding-the-homeless projects? Relationships built around task and service are often the most lasting.

As we attempt to create more holistic avenues for our kids' faith, let's also ask the question, "What really constitutes healthy families?" Is it the typical but increasingly mythical pattern (i.e., successful Dad, at-home Mom, a house from *Better Homes and Gardens*, church every Sunday like clockwork)? Sometimes what constitutes health includes a jarring, paradigm-changing dose of struggle, crisis, hardship, fracture, and doubt. Can we as leaders make room for families that are going through difficult life situations (divorce, separation, unemployment, terminal illness, loss of faith and hope)? Can we actively aid them in their process instead of labeling them substandard? Let's face it: some of the strongest teens come from the most difficult family contexts.

Sally Morgenthaler

This kind of simplified living will be a great witness in the postmodern world. To do this we'll have to overcome guilt and feelings of inadequacy that come when ours isn't the biggest youth group in town. And we'll have to look for churches that value well-balanced pastors. We'll have to explain to the committee that we only work three nights a week. We'll have to ask for a membership at the health club as part of the compensation package — and then have someone hold us accountable to actually go!

In an era of incredible wealth and information overload we can be the new monks — the ones who have stepped out of the world's frenetic pace in order to show that there is a different way. By doing so, not only will we last much longer in ministry, but also many lost, postmodern souls will come knocking on our doors, asking if they, too, can escape the world's madness.

epilogue

230 Some say postmodern thought and culture will run out of gas in just a few years. But I believe postmodernism is a force with staying power, a force to be reckoned with – one that is changing the course of the Western world.

And some say there's no good reason to apply this fairly ethereal theory to the day-to-day practice of Christian youth ministry. But I say that even if every kid in your youth group is modern, there's a big postmodern world waiting outside the doors of your church and your town. It won't be long before those modern students get deconstructed by postmodern movies, music, TV shows, and professors.

America at the end of the 20th century is fundamentally a society in transition. It is far from clear what kind of society we will have in the next century. One thing is clear, the search for community and for **the sacred will continue to characterize** the American people.

231

the sacred will continue to characterize

the American people.

Robert Wuthnow quoted in Jimmy Long, *Generating Hope: A Strategy for Reaching the Postmodern Generation*, 136

What can we do? We can be wise and help our students extricate their faith from their epistemology. That way, although their modernism is deconstructed, their faith won't be.

Postmodernism is neither something to fear nor something to embrace. It's simply the water in which we swim now. We will do well to read about it, observe it, and do our best to understand it.

This book may have made you excited, confused, or angry. You may have found the thoughts ludicrous or enlightening. In any case, I hope this foray into postmodernism and how it intersects with youth ministry is only a beginning, and that you will pick up some more books on the subject and join the conversation.

May God bless you in your ministry.

End Notes

1. "Cisco - Are You Ready? Children." Advertisement. Available on AdCritic.com Web site at http://www.adcritic.com/content/cisco-are-you-ready-children.html.

2. "Cisco - Are You Ready? Older Generation." Advertisement. Available on AdCritic.com Web site at http://www.adcritic.com/content/cisco-are-you-ready.html.

3. Stanley Grenz's book, *A Primer on Postmodernism* (Grand Rapids: Eerdmans, 1996) is an excellent introductory work on the philosophical trends that have led up to and include postmodernism. He looks at postmodernism from a Christian perspective and makes some very difficult philosophy understandable.

4. Nancey Murphy and James Wm. McLendon, "Distinguishing Modern and Postmodern Theologies" in *Modern Theology*, 5:3 (April, 1989), 193.

5. This diagram is thanks to Professor Nancey Murphy of Fuller Theological Seminary and her graduate seminar entitled "Theological Uses for Postmodern Philosophy" which I took in the spring of 1993. Murphy's classes and informal conversations are the impetus for much of my thinking on postmodernism, and this book is really an attempt to apply the thinking of people like Nancey Murphy and Stanley Grenz to youth ministry.

6. Albert Schweitzer, *The Quest for the Historical Jesus* (London: Adam & Charles Black, 1954).

7. Murphy and McLendon, 200.

8. For an excellent synopsis of postmodernism's credos, see Karen Endicott, "Post-What?" *Dartmouth Alumni Magazine*, December, 1998: 38-41.

9. In *After Virtue*, Alasdair MacIntyre makes an important distinction and correction: in fact, he argues, we do not live in a pluralistic world but a fragmented world. A pluralistic world would mean competing religious and philosophical worldviews are coherent. In fact, most postmodern thinkers repudiate the whole "worldview" concept because people are synthesizing a variety of beliefs into their system, and they hold only fragments of any one system.

10. The Cambridge Medieval History, 4; *Oxford Dictionary*, 1090.

11. Thomas S. Kuhn, *The Copernican Revolution* (Cambridge: Harvard University, 1957), 196, 199.

12. New York Times Service, "400 years after he died a heretic, philosopher is celebrated in Rome," *Minneapolis StarTribune*, February 18, 2000, A10.

13. Stanley Hauerwas and William H. Willimon, *Resident Aliens: Life in the Christian Colony* (Nashville: Abingdon, 1989), 15, 16.

14. "Mission Statement," The Center for Reclaiming America, Ft. Lauderdale, Florida. Available on the Internet at http://www.reclaimamerica.org/pages/mission.html.

15. Rodney Clapp, *A Peculiar People* (Downers Grove: InterVarsity Press, 1996), 16-23.

16. "Religion," The Gallup Organization, Princeton, New Jersey. Available on the Internet at http://www.gallup.com/poll/indicators/indreligion.asp.

17. George Gallup, Jr., "As Nation Observes National Day of Prayer, 9 in 10 Pray – 3 in 4 Daily," Poll Releases (May 6, 1999). The Gallup Organization, Princeton, New Jersey. Available on the Internet at http://www.gallup.com/poll/releases/pr990506.asp.

18. George Barna, "Teenagers Embrace Religion but Are Not Excited About Christianity," Barna Research Online, January 10, 2000. Available on the Internet at http://216.87.179.136/cgi-bin/PagePressRelease.asp?PressReleaseID=45&Reference=B.

19. On the idea of cultural chaplaincy, see Clapp, 16ff.

20. See their excellent Web site, designed by the kids: www.dinomights.com/home.htm

21a. "The Priest's Service Book," SS Peter & Paul Orthodox Church, Meriden, Connecticut. Available on the Internet at http://www.sspeterpaul.org/priest.html.

21. Miroslav Volf, *After Our Likeness: The Church as the Image of the Trinity* (Grand Rapids: Eerdmans, 1998), 2.

22. See *Youthworker* journal, March/April 2000, for an excellent issue on Reinforcing Theology. The interview with Kenda Creasy Dean is especially good.

23. Em Griffin, *The Mind Changers* (Wheaton: Tyndale, 1976), cover, 29.

24. James Olson and Raymond Wilson, *Native Americans in the Twentieth Century* (Urbana: University of Illinois, 1984), 29, 49.

25. Milton L. Rudnick, *Speaking the Truth through the Ages: A History of Evangelism* (St. Louis: Concordia, 1984), 199. Cited in Wilbert R. Shenk, *Write the Vision: The Church Renewed* (Harrisburg: Trinity, 1995), 66.

26. Shenk, 62.

27. Dallas Willard, *The Divine Conspiracy: Rediscovering Our Hidden Life in God* (San Francisco: Harper, 1998), 11.

28. Shenk, 62

29. Griffin, 36.

30. Mark Yaconelli, "Youth Ministry: A Contemplative Approach" in *Christian Century*, April 21-28, 1999.

31. Willard Van Orman Quine, *From a Logical Point of View* (Cambridge: Harvard, 1953), 42. Italics mine.

32. Although Quine was writing primarily about science, his work has been applied across many fields – notably in Christian theology by Nancey Murphy of Fuller Seminary and a few other Christian philosophers.

33. Quine, 42.

34. Quine, 43.

35. "Disciple," *The American Heritage Dictionary of the English Language,* 3rd ed. (New York: Houghton Mifflin, 1996). Available online at http://www.dictionary.com/cgi-bin/dict.pl?term=disciple.

36. The details of this section were gleaned from The Internet Dictionary of Philosophy.

37. Ludwig Wittgenstein, *The Blue and Brown Books* (New York: Harper, 1965), 42. Italics added.

38. Murphy and McClendon, 202.

39. George Lindbeck, *The Nature of Doctrine* (Philadelphia: Westminster, 1984). While some believe Lindbeck's post-liberal (he uses this term interchangeably with "postmodern") theological viewpoint is mutually exclusive of evangelical theology, I strongly disagree. For the best discussion of this debate, see Timothy R. Phillips and Dennis L. Okham, eds., *The Nature of Confession: Evangelicals and Postliberals in Conversation* (Downers Grove: InterVarsity Press, 1996), a summation of a dialogue held at Wheaton College in 1995.

40. Lindbeck, 33. Italics added.

41. See Marva Dawn, *Reaching Out without Dumbing Down* (Grand Rapids: Eerdmans, 1995).

42. Lindbeck, 132. Italics added.

43. Louis Berkhof, *Systematic Theology* (Grand Rapids: Eerdmans, 1939), 513.

44. For this fictional account, I am indebted to Richard Osmer's *Confirmation: Presbyterian Practices in Ecumenical Perspective* (Louisville: Geneva, 1996) 29-58; *The Oxford Dictionary of the Christian Church*, 395-397; and to Professor Edward Bradley of Dartmouth College with whom I have been to Italy four times.

45. Osmer, 40. Italics added. He notes that prior to Constantine's conversion, possibly one-fourth of the Roman Empire had already converted to Christianity.

46. Osmer, xii, xiii.

47. Osmer, 91.

48. The mentoring aspect of our confirmation program is introduced by Hauerwas and Willimon in *Resident Aliens* and spelled out by William Willimon in *Making Disciples.*

49. *The Spiritual Exercises of St. Ignatius of Loyola,* translated by Father Elder Mullan, S.J. Calvin College, Grand Rapids, Michigan. Available on the Internet at http://www.ccel.org/i/ignatius/exercises/exercises.html.

50. "Lectio Divina: About Lectio Divina," Order of Saint Benedict, Inc., Collegeville, Minnesota (6 November 2000). Available on the Internet at http://www.osb.org/lectio/about.html.

51. "Labyrinth," GraceCathedral.org (San Francisco: Grace Cathedral, 2000). Available on the Internet at http://www.gracecathedral.org/labyrinth/index.shtml. Grace Cathedral has led the North American rediscovery of labyrinth.

52. "Propaganda." *The American Heritage Dictionary of the English Language,* 3rd ed. (New York: Houghton Mifflin, 1996). Available on the Internet at http://www.dictionary.com/cgi-bin/dict.pl?term=propaganda.

53. Timothy R. Phillips and Dennis L. Okham, eds., *The Nature of Confession: Evangelicals and Postliberals in Conversation* (Downers Grove: InterVarsity Press, 1996), 9.

54. Phillips and Okham, 9.

55. Phillips and Okham, 11.

56. With apologies to Nancey Murphy, who wrote *Beyond Liberalism and Fundamentalism* (Trinity, 1996).

57. George Lindbeck, "The Church's Mission to a Postmodern Culture" in *Postmodern Theology*, edited by Frederic B. Burnham (San Francisco: Harper Collins, 1989), 41.

58. Lindbeck, 52.

59. Alasdair MacIntyre, *After Virtue* (Notre Dame: University of Notre Dame, 1984), 34.

60. MacIntyre, 69.

61. MacIntyre, 187.

62. MacIntyre, 219.

List of Works Consulted

The American Heritage Dictionary of the English Language. 3rd edition. New York: Houghton Mifflin, 1996. Available online at http://www.dictionary.com/cgi-bin/dict.pl?term=.

Burnham, Frederic B., ed., *Postmodern Theology: Christian Faith in a Pluralist World*, San Francisco: Harper, 1989. Burnham collected a series essays by leading thinkers in the early days of postmodern theology, including an excellent essay by George Lindbeck, "The Church's Mission to a Postmodern World."

Caputo, John D., ed., *Deconstruction in a Nutshell: A Conversation with Jacques Derrida,* New York: Fordham, 1997. Jacques Derrida is the pioneer of deconstructionist thinking, and his writing is notoriously dense. But he seems much more understandable in a dialogical setting. This book is the result of a dialogue that took place at a roundtable discussion at Villanova University in 1994, edited with expertise and wit by John Caputo. See also Caputo's The Prayers and Tears of Jacques Derrida: Religion without Religion (Bloomington: Indiana University Press, 1979).

Clapp, Rodney, *A Peculiar People: The Church as Culture in a Post-Christian Society,* Downers Grove: InterVarsity, 1996. Clapp has a keen understanding of evangelicalism in North America, including its triumphs and foibles. In *A Peculiar People* he writes constructively about what the church is called to in the post-Constantinian world. This is a book about the geography of the land our students are being raised in, making it a must-read.

Dean, Kenda Creasy and Ron Foster, *The Godbearing Life: The Art of Soul Tending in Youth Ministry*, Nashville: Upper Room, 1998. A different kind of youth ministry book. It isn't about programming and ideas but about what it takes to care for kids' souls. Written from a mainline Protestant perspective, the authors deal with the spiritual formation of youth and their pastors.

Endicott, Karen, "Post-What?" *Dartmouth Alumni Magazine* (December 1998).

Grenz, Stanley, *A Primer on Postmodernism*, Grand Rapids: Eerdmans, 1996. Quite simply the most readable survey text on post-modernism written from an evangelical perspective.

Grenz, Stanley and John R. Franke, *Beyond Foundationalism: Shaping Theology in a Postmodern Context*, Louisville: Westminster John Knox, 2001. Moving beyond Enlightenment foundationalism that shaped modern theology, Franke and Grenz attempt to develop a holistic, Trinitarian theology that reflects postmodern methods.

Griffin, Em, *The Mind Changers: The Art of Christian Persuasion*, Wheaton: Tyndale, 1976. It's out of print, but if you can get a copy, it's worth it. Griffin has a very honest approach to evangelism that's highly applicable to the postmodern context. His critique of many modern youth evangelism techniques is devastating.

Hauerwas, Stanley and William H. Willimon, *Resident Aliens: Life in the Christian Colony*, Nashville: Abingdon, 1989. *The* classic in the discussion of how Christians are to interact with culture in a post-Christian world. Hauerwas and Willimon have keen insight into the cultural changes that took place in the second half of the 20th century and how the church must respond.

Kuhn, Thomas S., *The Copernican Revolution: Planetary Astronomy in the Development of Western Thought*, Cambridge: Harvard University, 1957. Kuhn's first rollout of the "paradigm shift" as it applied to cosmology.

Kuhn, Thomas S., *The Structure of Scientific Revolutions*, Chicago: University of Chicago, 1962. A watershed in Western thought and hailed as the most important work on the nature of rationality since Descartes, this essay has affected virtually every field of study. Kuhn dissects "paradigm shifts," showing that they take place by revolution, not evolution. That is, changes in thought and practice happen subjectively and somewhat chaotically. Though Kuhn does not necessarily claim that his ideas apply to theology and ministry, many others have.

Lindbeck, George, *The Nature of Doctrine: Religion and Theology in a Postliberal Age*, Philadelphia: Westminster, 1984. Possibly the most significant book written on biblical scholarship in the last century, Lindbeck critiques liberal and conservative hermeneutics with a novel, postmodern approach. He argues that Scripture is always read and understood in a cultural-linguistic context; that is, as part of the language of the church. See also Hans Frei, *The Eclipse of Biblical Narrative*, New Haven: Yale, 1980.

Long, Jimmy, *Generating Hope: A Strategy for Reaching the Postmodern Generation*, Downer's Grove: InterVarsity, 1997. More practical than theoretical, Long draws on his years of college campus ministry in developing strategies reach primarily Gen-Xers.

MacIntyre, Alasdair, *After Virtue: A Study in Moral Theory* (2nd edition), Notre Dame, IN: Notre Dame, 1984. Hailed as the most important work of philosophy in years, MacIntyre calls into question the disjointed conversation that is contemporary moral philosophy. As a corrective, he proposes a return to a interrelated system of virtues and practices, always embedded in a local narrative. He argues further for the cogency and coherence of his system in a relativistic world in *Whose Justice? Which Rationality?*, Notre Dame, Indiana: Notre Dame, 1989.

McClendon, James Wm., Jr., *Biography as Theology*, Philadelphia: Trinity, 1990. A "minor classic" in narrative theology, McLendon uses the lives of four modern day "saints" (Dag Hammarskjöld, Martin Luther King, Jr., Clarence Jordan, and Charles Ives) to shed light on particular biblical doctrines. Breaking with the norm of "systematic theology," McClendon uses the story of each person to elucidate the truth of Scripture. See also McClendon's three volumes of constructive theology: *Ethics* (1988), *Doctrine* (1994), and *Witness* (2000).

Murphy, Nancey, *Beyond Liberalism and Fundamentalism: How Modern and Postmodern Philosophy Set the Theological Agenda*, Harrisburg, Pennsylvania: Trinity, 1996. The Fuller Seminary professor first shows conclusively how modern theologies, both conservative (as represented by Charles Hodge and Benjamin Warfield) and liberal (as represented by Frederich Schleiermacher) are utterly dependent upon the foundationalist philosophy of Descartes, Locke, and Hume. She then proceeds to draw upon the work of George Lindbeck, Alasdair MacIntyre, and other postmodern thinkers to develop a nonfoundationalist theology that cannot be bifurcated into "left" and "right."

Murphey, Nancey and James Wm. McClendon, "Distinguishing Modern and Postmodern Theologies" in *Modern Theology*, 5:3 (April 1989). In this essay, the authors lay out the different axes of modern and postmodern thought and show how they affect the theologies associated with them.

Newbigin, Lesslie, *Foolishness to the Greeks: The Gospel and Western Culture*, Grand Rapids: Eerdmans, 1986. After 40 years as a missionary in India, Newbigin returned to England and the United States to find a culture that had forsaken the gospel message. With the perspective of a missionary from the outside looking in, Newbigin asks how biblical authority can confront Western society. His challenge to the church is to be missional, even in the West, and he continues that call in *The Gospel in a Pluralist Society*, Grand Rapids: Eerdmans, 1989.

Osmer, Richard, *Confirmation: Presbyterian Practices in Ecumenical Perspective*. Louisville: Geneva, 1996.

Phillips, Timothy R. and Dennis L. Okham, eds., *The Nature of Confession: Evangelicals and Postliberals in Conversation*, Downers Grove: InterVarsity Press, 1996. This is the compilation of essays presented at a conference at Wheaton College in 1995. A variety of authors the "Yale School" of postmodern biblical scholarship and from evangelicalism debate about the resonance and applicability of George Lindbeck's work. It's an excellent volume that helps parse out many of the particulars of Lindbeck's program.

Placher, William C., *Unapologetic Theology: A Christian Voice in a Pluralistic Conversation*, Louisville: Westminster/John Knox, 1989. Applying postmodern philosophy to theology, Placher takes on the challenge of engaging foundationalism, science, anthropology, and theological method – an excellent translation of new ideas into the theological realm.

Quine, Willard Van Orman, *From a Logical Point of View*, Cambridge: Harvard, 1953. Quine develops a devastating critique of the reductionism of Locke and Hume, who believed that all truth and knowledge could be boiled down a universal experience shared by all human beings. Instead, Quine argues, truth is known in a network of beliefs, constructed by communities of individuals. See also *Word and Object*, Cambridge: M.I.T., 1964.

Schweitzer, Albert, *The Quest for the Historical Jesus*. London: Adam & Charles Black, 1954.

Shenk, Wilbert R., *Write the Vision: The Church Renewed*, Harrisburg, Pennsylvania: Trinity, 1995. The Christian Mission and Modern Culture series is about a dozen short books (about 100 pages each) that deal with the mission of the postmodern church. All are readable and could be discussed by lay people and clergy alike.

Volf, Miroslav, *After Our Likeness: The Church as the Image of the Trinity*, Grand Rapids: Eerdmans, 1998. After a long dry spell, evangelical theologians are beginning to deal with ecclesiology. Here Volf suggests that the church take its form from the community that is Father, Son, and Holy Spirit and "converses" with the writings of a preeminent Roman Catholic theologian (Joseph Cardinal Ratzinger) and an Orthodox theologian (metropolitan John Zizioulas) – thereby setting for us an excellent example of ecumenical dialogue.

Webber, Robert E., *Ancient-Future Faith: Rethinking Evangelicalism for a Postmodern World*, Grand Rapids: Baker, 1999. Webber answers the question "What will the future of Christianity look like?" by looking to the church of the past. Shedding modern categories, he looks at Christ, the church, worship, spirituality, and mission – learning from the past and keeping an eye on the future.

Willard, Dallas, *The Divine Conspiracy: Rediscovering Our Hidden Life in God*, San Francisco: Harper, 1998. Willard's highly renowned book takes a fresh look at the Sermon on the Mount and what it takes to live as a Christian disciple, with integrity, in today's world.

Wittgenstein, Ludwig, *The Blue and Brown Books*. New York: Harper, 1965.

Yaconelli, Mike, "What Would Jesus Say?" in *Youthworker* journal, January/February 2000. Youth workers are blessed six times a year when they flip to the back page of *Youthworker* to read Yaconelli's column, "Dangerous Wonder." It is always insightful, often witty, and very challenging. Give a copy to your youth committee!

The postmodern reply to the modern consists of recognizing that the past—since it cannot really be destroyed, because its destruction leads to silence—must be revisited:

but with irony, not innocently.

Umberto Eco, postscript to *The Name of the Rose*, 530

Resources from Youth Specialties

Youth Ministry Programming

Camps, Retreats, Missions, & Service Ideas (Ideas Library)
Compassionate Kids: Practical Ways to Involve Your Students in Mission and Service
Creative Bible Lessons from the Old Testament
Creative Bible Lessons in 1 & 2 Corinthians
Creative Bible Lessons in John: Encounters with Jesus
Creative Bible Lessons in Romans: Faith on Fire!
Creative Bible Lessons on the Life of Christ
Creative Bible Lessons in Psalms
Creative Junior High Programs from A to Z, Vol. 1 (A-M)
Creative Junior High Programs from A to Z, Vol. 2 (N-Z)
Creative Meetings, Bible Lessons, & Worship Ideas (Ideas Library)
Crowd Breakers & Mixers (Ideas Library)
Downloading the Bible Leader's Guide
Drama, Skits, & Sketches (Ideas Library)
Drama, Skits, & Sketches 2 (Ideas Library)
Dramatic Pauses
Everyday Object Lessons
Games (Ideas Library)
Games 2 (Ideas Library)
Games 3 (Ideas Library)
Good Sex: A Whole-Person Approach to Teenage Sexuality & God
Great Fundraising Ideas for Youth Groups
More Great Fundraising Ideas for Youth Groups
Great Retreats for Youth Groups
Holiday Ideas (Ideas Library)
Hot Illustrations for Youth Talks
More Hot Illustrations for Youth Talks
Still More Hot Illustrations for Youth Talks
Ideas Library on CD-ROM
Incredible Questionnaires for Youth Ministry
Junior High Game Nights
More Junior High Game Nights
Kickstarters: 101 Ingenious Intros to Just about Any Bible Lesson
Live the Life! Student Evangelism Training Kit
Memory Makers
The Next Level Leader's Guide
Play It! Over 150 Great Games for Youth Groups
Roaring Lambs
So What Am I Gonna Do With My Life?
Special Events (Ideas Library)
Spontaneous Melodramas
Spontaneous Melodramas 2
Student Leadership Training Manual
Student Underground: An Event Curriculum on the Persecuted Church
Super Sketches for Youth Ministry
Talking the Walk
Teaching the Bible Creatively
Videos That Teach

What Would Jesus Do? Youth Leader's Kit
Wild Truth Bible Lessons
Wild Truth Bible Lessons 2
Wild Truth Bible Lessons—Pictures of God
Worship Services for Youth Groups

Professional Resources

Administration, Publicity, & Fundraising (Ideas Library)
Dynamic Communicators Workshop
Equipped to Serve: Volunteer Youth Worker Training Course
Help! I'm a Junior High Youth Worker!
Help! I'm a Small-Group Leader!
Help! I'm a Sunday School Teacher!
Help! I'm a Volunteer Youth Worker!
How to Expand Your Youth Ministry
How to Speak to Youth...and Keep Them Awake at the Same Time
Junior High Ministry (Updated & Expanded)
The Ministry of Nurture: A Youth Worker's Guide to Discipling Teenagers
Postmodern Youth Ministry
Purpose-Driven® Youth Ministry
Purpose-Driven® Youth Ministry Training Kit
So That's Why I Keep Doing This! 52 Devotional Stories for Youth Workers
A Youth Ministry Crash Course
Youth Ministry Management Tools
The Youth Worker's Handbook to Family Ministry

Academic Resources

Four Views of Youth Ministry & the Church
Starting Right: Thinking Theologically About Youth Ministry

Discussion Starters

Discussion & Lesson Starters (Ideas Library)
Discussion & Lesson Starters 2 (Ideas Library)
EdgeTV
Get 'Em Talking
Keep 'Em Talking!
Good Sex: A Whole-Person Approach to Teenage Sexuality & God
High School TalkSheets—Updated!
More High School TalkSheets—Updated!
High School TalkSheets from Psalms and Proverbs—Updated!
Junior High-Middle School TalkSheets—Updated!
More Junior High-Middle School TalkSheets—Updated!
Junior High-Middle School TalkSheets from Psalms and Proverbs—Updated!
Real Kids: Short Cuts
Real Kids: The Real Deal—on Friendship, Loneliness, Racism, & Suicide
Real Kids: The Real Deal—on Sexual Choices, Family Matters, & Loss

Real Kids: The Real Deal—on Stressing Out, Addictive Behavior, Great Comebacks, & Violence
Real Kids: Word on the Street
Unfinished Sentences: 450 Tantalizing Statement Starters to Get Teenagers Talking & Thinking
What If...? 450 Thought-Provoking Questions to Get Teenagers Talking, Laughing, and Thinking
Would You Rather...? 465 Provocative Questions to Get Teenagers Talking
Have You Ever...? 450 Intriguing Questions Guaranteed to Get Teenagers Talking

Art Source Clip Art

Stark Raving Clip Art (print)
Youth Group Activities (print)
Clip Art Library Version 2.0 (CD-ROM)

Digital Resources

Clip Art Library Version 2.0 (CD-ROM)
Ideas Library on CD-ROM
Youth Ministry Management Tools

Videos & Video Curricula

Dynamic Communicators Workshop
EdgeTV
Equipped to Serve: Volunteer Youth Worker Training Course
The Heart of Youth Ministry: A Morning with Mike Yaconelli
Live the Life! Student Evangelism Training Kit
Purpose-Driven® Youth Ministry Training Kit
Real Kids: Short Cuts
Real Kids: The Real Deal—on Friendship, Loneliness, Racism, & Suicide
Real Kids: The Real Deal—on Sexual Choices, Family Matters, & Loss
Real Kids: The Real Deal—on Stressing Out, Addictive Behavior, Great Comebacks, & Violence
Real Kids: Word on the Street
Student Underground: An Event Curriculum on the Persecuted Church
Understanding Your Teenager Video Curriculum
Youth Ministry Outside the Lines

Student Resources

Downloading the Bible: A Rough Guide to the New Testament
Downloading the Bible: A Rough Guide to the Old Testament
Grow For It Journal through the Scriptures
So What Am I Gonna Do With My Life?
Spiritual Challenge Journal: The Next Level
Teen Devotional Bible
What (Almost) Nobody Will Tell You about Sex
What Would Jesus Do? Spiritual Challenge Journal
Wild Truth Journal for Junior Highers
Wild Truth Journal—Pictures of God
Wild Truth Journal—Pictures of God 2